Schools That Dream

Shashi Velath is the CEO of Tinge of Green, an ecosystem enabler and builder within the sustainability solutions space. A renowned war and investigative journalist, he has earned prestigious awards such as the Ramnath Goenka Award and a Green Oscar. Transitioning into the social sector, he led international non-profits in fostering cross-sector collaborations and addressing complex societal challenges. With a passion for designing innovative strategies for sustainable development goals, Shashi now spearheads Tinge of Green's mission. The organisation focuses on fostering collaboration, innovation and growth within the sustainability sector through platforms, investment, partnerships, research support, policy advocacy, education and sustainability standards.

Anand Haridas, a seasoned news journalist, began his career with *The Hindu*, where he gained recognition for captivating features on arts, culture and civic affairs. After a fruitful fourteen-year tenure, he transitioned into a content curator and media consultant. An accomplished translator, his rendition of Sajitha Madathil's play *Kaali Naatakam* was published in *Indian Literature*, a prestigious journal by Kendra Sahitya Akademi. Notably, he also co-authored the acclaimed film *Viral Sebi* alongside Sajitha Madathil, directed by award-winning filmmaker Vidhu Vincent. Anand's poetry has graced numerous publications and he is a regular host of engaging online talk shows.

Schools That Dream

Transforming Kerala's Schools into Empathy Engines

Shashi Velath
& Anand Haridas

WESTLAND
NON·FICTION

First published by Westland Non-Fiction, an imprint of Westland Books, a division of Nasadiya Technologies Private Limited, in 2023

No. 269/2B, First Floor, 'Irai Arul', Vimalraj Street, Nethaji Nagar, Alapakkam Main Road, Maduravoyal, Chennai 600095

Westland, the Westland logo, Westland Non-Fiction and the Westland Non-Fiction logo are the trademarks of Nasadiya Technologies Private Limited, or its affiliates.

Copyright © Shashi Velath and Anand Haridas, 2023

ISBN: 9789357767576

Shashi Velath and Anand Haridas assert the moral right to be identified as the authors of this work.

10 9 8 7 6 5 4 3 2 1

The views and opinions expressed in this work are the authors' own and the facts are as reported by them, and the publisher is in no way liable for the same.

Typeset by Jojy Philip, New Delhi
Printed at Parksons Graphics Pvt. Ltd

Contents

Note from the Authors   vii

Section I
The Birth and Rise of SPC

1.   I Am the Solution   3

2.   From Shadows to Light   16

3.   Reimagining Schools as Changemaking Hubs   32

4.   A Humane Police: How SPC Transformed   46
     Kerala Police

5.   Positivity and Possibilities: SPC's Impact   63
     on Society

Section II
Success Stories of SPC

6.   Conserving the Future   75

7.   The Red Night in Forest   82

8.   That Long Beep in the Dark   88

9.   When Trees Rushed Down the Hill   97

10. Fruits of Labour 104

11. Designs of an Agonised Mind 110

12. I Am More Than a Stereotype 115

13. Hands to Serve and Heart to Love 120

14. Be the Change, Make the Change 124

15. The Elixir of Life 129

16. Words Beyond Silence 134

Section III
Praise for SPC

17. No Going Back *Muhammad Yunus* 141

18. Setting the tone for a Gender Equal World *Dr Yasmin Ali Haque* 147

19. The World's Largest School Transformation Programme *Manoj Kumar Jha* 157

Acknowledgements 162

Note from the Authors
Everyone's a Changemaker

On 2 August 2010, the Government of Kerala officially inaugurated a voluntary student organisation, the Student Police Cadet (SPC), that had a larger vision of blending the patriotic discipline of the National Cadet Corps (NCC) with the nation-building social commitment of the National Service Scheme (NSS). The SPC programme is a school-based educational initiative designed to train high school students to be responsible and socially committed individuals, willing and able to selflessly serve their community.

The larger aim of SPC is to enable young minds to evolve from the narrow perspective of civic duty to a wider understanding of responsible citizenship, thereby creating a law-abiding society rooted not in fear of the police or government agencies but in the rational outcome of civilised behaviour. The programme is jointly implemented by various departments of the Kerala government, essentially the departments of home and education, with support from the departments of local self-government, transport, excise, forest, sports and youth welfare and fire and rescue services.

The SPC movement has gained momentum over the last two decades and triggered a changemaker movement in 13,000 schools in India across eleven states, including 1,001 schools in Kerala. Currently, there are 88,000 students undergoing training and over 2,50,000 student cadets have completed training so far since 2010—these are just the numbers for Kerala. Overall, a million students are enrolled in this programme across the country who understand that, in a rapidly changing world, everyone must be a changemaker to effectively contribute to the good of all.

India is home to the world's largest youth population—one-third of the country's demographic is below the age of fourteen years, 50 per cent is below twenty-five years and 65 per cent is below thirty-five years. Therefore, school-level education in India must have the ability to transform young people into problem-solvers. The success of the SPC programme in Kerala, which reimagines schools as innovation hubs alongside their traditional role as learning centres, is now being sought to be replicated across India. On July 2018, the Government of India announced the national roll-out of SPC.

Schools That Dream is a book of stories of social transformation made possible under the SPC schools in Kerala. To understand why SPC is so successful, we need to step back and look at history as well. For many centuries, success meant efficiency in repetition; one became successful by closely observing and replicating the behaviour of those before us. People trained to acquire a certain skill, like accounting, mechanics and so on, and went to work in a world of walls that allowed them to repeat that skill for life. The world today has advanced a lot from the era in which this practice was viable.

In today's new reality, the world is becoming an ever more intricately interconnected and morphing medley of teams, and these teams need all their members to quickly see new value opportunities. Anyone without changemaking skills cannot play effectively and will swiftly be marginalised without exception. This trend is already evident across the planet with millions of people who do not understand the new game or do not have the necessary skills to adapt to it efficiently, falling off the edge of society.

The Industrial Revolution, which started in the late eighteenth century, dramatically increased the need for literacy. As societies became more industrialised, being able to read and write became essential for an increasing number of jobs. This was true not only for more specialised professions but also for everyday tasks like understanding instructions or navigating urban areas.

Moreover, the emphasis on pattern recognition and conformity in tasks and behaviours resonates with the increasing standardisation seen during the Industrial Revolution. The assembly line, for example, is a clear illustration of this, with each worker needed to perform a specific, repetitive task.

It's also worth noting that the idea of literacy has expanded in the modern digital age. Today, digital literacy and information literacy—the ability to understand and use information from a variety of digital sources—are as important as traditional reading and writing skills were during the Industrial Revolution. The historical trend towards conformity and behavioural patterns during the Industrial Revolution was essential for the functioning of industrialised societies. However, the twenty-first century, characterised by rapid technological progress and a shift towards knowledge-based economies, requires a different set of skills, such as empathy, creativity, collaboration, curiosity and self-leadership.

The first is empathy. As societies grew more interconnected and diverse, the ability to understand and share the feelings of others became increasingly important. In both personal and professional settings, empathy aids in conflict resolution, team building and the design of products and services that meet diverse needs.

The second is creativity. The standardisation that came with the Industrial Revolution has given way to a demand for innovative thinking. The ability to come up with unique solutions to complex problems is highly valued in the current era where change is a constant.

The third is collaboration. As tasks become more complex and specialised, the ability to work effectively in teams has become crucial. It is often necessary to collaborate with others to complete tasks that would be impossible for individuals working alone.

The fourth is curiosity. In an age of rapid technological and societal changes, the willingness to continually learn and adapt is essential. Curiosity drives individuals to explore new concepts, acquire new skills and stay abreast of the latest developments in their fields.

The last is self-leadership. As workplaces become more flexible and decentralised, the ability to self-direct and self-motivate is becoming increasingly important. It is often up to individuals to take the initiative in learning new skills, solving problems and organising their work.

Written literacy became a must for anyone wanting to excel in life around 150 years ago since it essentially prepared people to align with a pattern. In that environment, being able to read was a prerequisite for finding a place in the society, defined by activities like understanding street signs or instruction manuals to perform activities in a specific way to fulfil a specific purpose. In other words, conforming to an accepted pattern was the norm then.

But it is not so today. Everyone needs to be a changemaker by practising conscious empathy in their everyday life, being part of and contributing to teamwork, developing the ability to self-lead such that the focus is for the good of all and having deep self-belief in the idea that each one represents the possibilities of a solution.

We define a changemaker as someone who envisions a better reality, builds a team to realise this purpose and takes action to bring this reality into being, while continuously learning and adjusting for the good of all. We believe that changemakers come in all ages and excel at the following abilities:

Conscious Empathy: The ability to be aware of and understand differing perspectives, to use that understanding to recognise patterns over time and guide one's actions towards a purpose that contributes to the good of all.

Teamwork: The ability to contribute to and thrive in a fluid ecosystem of teams that mobilises around each new problem or opportunity.

Changemaking Leadership: A leadership mindset that recognises that in a world of constant change, the role is to envision, enable and then ensure that every player is an initiator and sees the big picture.

Changemaking Action: The process of creating a novel solution to a social problem that is more effective, efficient and sustainable than existing solutions and for which the value created accrues primarily to society rather than to private individuals.

To envision and build a world in which everyone is a changemaker and everyone is powerful, it is critical to be actively committed to the good of all and possess the skills to contribute positively in personal and social settings. There are many ways to help young children master living for the good of all. Around the age of eleven, children transition from being a child to a young person. At this point, it is critical to help all young people be and practice being changemakers. The world does not operate in isolation anymore. Individual excellences are overridden by collective efforts—children need to learn the power of collaborative thinking. The smooth and responsible transition between these two stages of life is critical today and will remain so in the future.

For every child to be a changemaker, it is important to build this idea into all aspects of youth culture—at school, at youth programmes and in the workplace. This is where SPC has stepped in and taken the responsibility of enabling and empowering young children in their transition to young changemakers. SPC schools have changed the framework of education across society. The principals of schools associated with SPC realise that their success as educators is based on their students grasping this most critical foundational skill of being individual changemakers working together to usher in progress that is more than the sum of its individual parts.

Schools That Dream captures this courageous resolution of SPC schools that inspire their students to practice 'changemaking' just as they practice math, science, geography or any other curricular subject in and out of school. SPC training is provided across seven dimensions: physical, emotional, ethical, thinking, enterprise, societal and environmental.

When children see and identify a problem or opportunity, they allow themselves to imagine a solution, envision it in action, go out and build a team to make the solution and then persevere and persist until that vision becomes a new reality in their school or community. It is then that they have gained a power that they will possess for the rest of their life.

These reasons explain why society must now apply two key measures to promote a changemaking culture.

- What percentage of teenagers recognise themselves as changemakers?
- How many stakeholders in a school community can accurately identify whether they have a successful program based on its alignment with a proactive 'changemaker' culture?

Both are measures of mindset change. We must change mindsets to embrace the new reality of changemaking and forge new forms of leadership. We would be successful when parents interviewing the principal of a school where they intend to send their child ask with barely concealed excitement 'What proportion of your kids know they are changemakers and at what level?' and both sides know that the right answer (and the truthful one at that) is the majority.

The entire world now needs to know the new game—the new changemaking and innovation culture introduced by SPC in schools in Kerala. *Schools That Dream* shows the roadmap that all schools across the world must implement as we enter the post-pandemic world. It is with great excitement that we anticipate the far-reaching and incredible transformations new changemakers born out of SPC are sure to bring to the second decade of the millennium. This is Inspector General Puthiyottil Vijayan's magnificent vision of schools as innovation hubs producing conscious, compassionate, caring and responsible citizens, which is now being realised in 13,000 schools across India and beyond.

This motivates us to dream about an India where every young person says, 'I am the solution.'

Shashi Velath and Anand Haridas

Section I
The Birth and Rise of SPC

1

I Am the Solution

Can we imagine schools as spaces where young people are able to reflect? It will always be a space for learning. What else can it be? Through SPC, we demonstrated that we can transform schools to be spaces where children can reflect and act. They are enabled and empowered to reflect on questions, like, 'How do I change the world for the better?' For instance, one SPC student, Anshida, during the pandemic, came across an aged couple without access to water. She reflected on this issue and mobilised her family and the local community to set up a water pipeline connection for the couple. Or take the example of SPC students at Vithura, near Trivandrum, who set up a biodiversity park in the land allotted to them within a police station. Within the SPC school ecosystem, students are being given a chance to reflect on and act on the question 'How do I change the world for the better?' by taking small steps.

There is a difference between 'spectating' and conscious leadership. The former is when a person concerned about an issue preaches solutions and there is zero involvement in solving a problem. SPC students are, on the contrary, problem-solvers. They display conscious leadership abilities that help them to identify and map the problem, explore the best course of action, brainstorm, reflect and act upon it.

Over the past fifteen years, SPC students have learnt that it does not serve them or their communities if they remain bystanders. They learnt that their acts of leadership can positively transform them, their families and their communities.

If every young person in India sees themself as part of the solution or the solution itself, imagine the shift in perspective! Indeed, every young person in India is a changemaker. This is the next stage for channelising the energy of young India and instilling the belief in every young Indian that 'I am the solution.'

The words 'I am the solution' creates a compelling need for inward reflection. What am I solving? What solution am I bringing to the table? The value of SPC is that it distributed the ability to solve at scale. SPC has created an ecosystem where the fundamental thing a young person learns is the belief in their ability to solve problems.

What is the role the youth can play in helping society better organise itself in a world of increasingly rapid change? The accelerated rate of change that we are witnessing in this era is staggering. As George Bernard Shaw wrote: 'Progress is impossible without change, and those who cannot change their minds cannot change anything.'

The changemaking capacity of young people has been astonishing. During the pandemic, student police cadets took on the role of educators and provided phone counselling to their peers stuck at home because of lockdowns. This is a great example of how they supported their communities and society at large. Through the Kutty Desk (Children's Desk) project, student police cadets were able to bring mental health awareness to their parents.

Then there is the Feed A Stomach programme, which was conceived during the pandemic as a community intervention in Kerala to feed homeless people, family bystanders at hospitals, patients in hospitals and all frontline staff, including emergency and health workers. Obviously, it was extremely difficult for them to access regular meals during the lockdown. It was important they were well looked after. The SPC directorate was in regular touch with cadets across all SPC schools via online meetings. The question posed to youngsters was simply: How do we feed homeless people and frontline COVID-19 warriors?

The children responded with solutions. They organised their home kitchens to make food packets and used the police machinery to distribute the food. Soon, they inspired local communities across various cities and towns to organise similar community kitchens. They also started donation drives and encouraged their families to contribute raw materials to community kitchens. The cadets coordinated with local police stations for the direct distribution of food packets to those in need. Overall, around a million high-quality and tasty home-cooked food packets were distributed across Kerala during the lockdown.

The programme wasn't merely about distributing food to the needy. It was about food cooked with love and care. It was a new learning: if educators can impart value-based education and provide opportunities for young people to practice empathetic changemaking, then they display a natural ability to collaborate and solve problems.

There is another incredible example of successful collaboration by the young changemakers in Kerala. After the lockdown was lifted, schools opened in online mode. Thousands of disadvantaged children were unable to access online classrooms. In June 2020, a school TV channel, Victers, began broadcasting classroom sessions for children without access to the internet.

Youngsters were confronted with the challenge of supporting students who didn't have TV sets at home. Guess what happened next? The SPC youngsters ran a campaign from their homes and were able to mobilise 6,000 TV sets and distribute thousands of mobile phone connections for internet connectivity. The scale at which the cadets were able to organise and operate was stunning.

It is vital to understand this was happening in the middle of a raging pandemic. Thousands of school students joined a campaign, mobilising their friends, family, relatives and neighbours through phone calls. This was compassion in action. They were running the campaign from homes by mobilising everyone they knew. They did not have the freedom to go out of their homes to collect donations. The Kutty Desk, a peer-to-peer phone counselling service designed and operated by the students, proved to be useful in this campaign.

The first-hand impact of SPC was clear to see. This was a changemaking generation in action. We must have full belief in the ability of young people to organise and respond to situations. Parents and teachers are responsible for providing mentorship.

Children are natural systems thinkers—all they need is an enabling environment. Whether it is feeding thousands of hungry stomachs or mobilising 6,000 TV sets, they know how to bring various stakeholders together in an organic way, with appropriate guidance and mentorship.

At times, they may not be able to see an issue in its entirety, and that is understandable. If you give them a task, they have a sense of purpose to directly seek a solution without any constraints. For instance, in the case of mobilising TV sets, several children who had two TV sets at home decided to give away one without even asking their parents.

For the Feed A Stomach programme, twenty-six community kitchens across Kerala were set up. By around 10.30 a.m., children would be queuing up in front of kitchens with vegetables, grocery items, money—whatever they could mobilise from their homes. They were not worried about if their parents approved or not. The objective of SPC is to instil within them a culture of social service. When the task is clear, the children are clear about their roles as well.

In Kerala, nearly fourteen government departments along with school administrations, parent–teacher associations (PTAs) and the local parent community come together to make SPC successful. Without parents being interested and invested in what happens at schools, it would not have been possible to create the changemaking ecosystem that SPC is today.

For example, there is a school-level advisory committee, Guardian SPC, that brings together the parents of SPC students. Through these mechanisms, deep socialistic values at SPC were nurtured—its activities and their benefits for students and society, how it will positively impact students and change their lives and why this should be part of an effective education system.

Initially, it was not easy to change the mindset of parents. However, the enthusiasm, infectious energy and positive change in behavioural patterns of the youngsters made social acceptance of SPC possible.

There are many small, but significant changemaking activities SPC students are engaged with.

There is a beautiful concept called 'My Tree, My Dream'. Generally, the afforestation campaign or social forestry campaign is focused on planting trees. Every year on 5 June, a large number of trees are planted. But nobody bothers with what happens to these trees after being planted. Are they nurtured and taken care of? These questions were raised during a review. This lacunae in the programme had to be resolved. In SPC schools, there are numerous clubs: Road Safety Club, Anti-Narcotic Club, and the Literary Club. These clubs hold programmes occasionally but there is hardly any continuity and so the programmatic impact was minimal. The truth is that mere awareness programmes do not make a big difference in the lives of people.

The conclusion was that it is necessary to create a deep-rooted impact on the personality and mindset of the students. To achieve this, we must put in place a system of consistent training, enabling them to evolve as responsible and capable citizens.

My Tree, My Dream became one of SPC's most successful campaigns and an effective climate-friendly intervention because we made sure that each student understood what it means to take responsibility of a tree. The cadets were told, 'You are responsible for your tree until it grows up.'

Nearly two million trees were planted in 2022 across Kerala. SPC has contributed to offsetting approximately 50,000 tonnes of CO_2 this year. Isn't this a fabulous achievement? Shouldn't it be replicated across all states in India? It is entirely possible for each young person in India to be a changemaker is such projects.

Through SPC, we instil a sense of responsibility in young people to take ownership of what they wish to change within themselves. Without a sense of responsibility, no action can be taken. An ecosystem must be created to ensure that this sense of responsibility is taken forward sustainably through wilful volunteerism—not compulsion. For instance, in the My Tree, My Dream campaign, the core philosophy was that if you nurture a tree, you must nurture it through your entire school journey. It is your responsibility to look after the tree you planted. We connected this responsibility to their dream of what they aspired to solve as adults. We told them that just as they nurture their aspirations, they should do for the tree. 'Nurture the tree you plant, be responsible for it and you will eventually realise your dream.'

The students were also encouraged to inculcate a questioning mind. '*Why* should I take the responsibility to nurture a tree?' This allows them to go on an immersive journey of self-discovery on why they should protect trees and what they are going to contribute to do so. We enable them to see the change they are bringing. They make strong emotional connections. This leads to wilful acceptance of responsibility; otherwise, it becomes an imposition of the same. After this is achieved, the SPC ecosystem constantly encourages school students to stay connected with their changemaking actions.

The primary focus is also to create an inherent respect for the law. There is one aspect of everyday life in India that makes everyone's lives miserable and that is the complete disregard for the law of the land. This creates chaos in every citizen's life, which is completely avoidable.

There is a feeling in large sections of the citizenry that the law is to be violated to the extent that it has now become the culture. These people can't connect with the utility of the idea that following the law is an important aspect of being a good citizen and fully participating in a democracy. After all, the law is enacted of the people, by the people and for the people in a democracy. If citizens fail to own the law they enact, how will the law operate in a democracy? The scripture for democracy is its constitution. It is the ultimate book of law in a democratic society. Unfortunately, an overwhelming majority of citizens have no understanding of this.

We are trying to create a community of young Indians who are fully conscious of the importance and utility of the rule of law. If everyone is law-abiding, we will be able to create a peaceful society that shuns violence and corruption. And, by doing this, we create a culture in which young people understand that the law is for their own safety and freedom.

No child should grow up in an atmosphere fearing the law. Instead, they should respect it. At SPC, early inculcation of this knowledge is practised and this is the core reason why this programme has had such a deep impact on society.

There is an SPC programme on road safety called Shubha Yathra, under which five major and recurring violations leading to the most accidents in the state were identified: not wearing seat belts, not using helmets while driving two-wheelers, drunken driving, pedestrians avoiding footpaths and walking on the wrong side of the road and pedestrians disregarding crossings and signals. One of the most frequent traffic violations in Kerala is helmetless driving.

The average annual death toll due to road accidents in Kerala is over 4,000. Two-wheeler accidents account for half of these deaths and 85 per cent of these deaths are because of head injuries. Statistics show that in most cases, the accidents took away the prime breadwinner. This led to an enormous imposition of trauma on the family, especially in the lives of children.

Road safety advocacy by the cadets is having a tremendous impact on society. Cadets speak to the motorists on the road, educate them on road safety and if they see a violation, they issue a warning. There is a strong focus on making them understand *why* these five traffic violations are dangerous for motorists and pedestrians alike.

Children are not being taught that drunken driving is a violation of Section 185 of the Motor Vehicle Act. Instead, they are made to understand why drunken driving is dangerous. They are told that when a driver is drunk, his motor skills are impaired; there is decreased concentration and vision, slow reaction time and poor judgement. The children understand and imbibe fully the message. The driving force of the campaign is 'Each One, Teach Ten'. Through children, we are raising awareness in society on how such offences contribute to fatal road accidents.

The beauty of the Subha Yathra road safety campaign is that it is a positive reinforcement campaign. On rare occasions when cadets observe a driver following the rules, they will hand over a toffee to them as a 'reward'. They also carry a red card for those who are in complete violation of the law and a yellow card for minor infringements or slight deviations. In reality, red cards are never issued, even to those who violate the law completely. They exist only in principle. Instead, they issue a yellow card as a warning, telling them, 'You won't be here to receive the red card if you continue violating the law.' It is a powerful message.

Once, a school principal sent a letter to the SPC directorate saying, 'I never used a helmet till I met the SPC students. They changed my perspective and from that day onwards, every time I ride my two-wheeler, I ensure that I wear the helmet.'

Another eventful incident is how a group of three cadets flagged down a family on a two-wheeler. None of the family members had a helmet on.

'What will happen if we don't wear helmets?' they asked the girls aggressively.

As the three students calmly waited for the family to cool down, one of them broke into a sob. 'Look at me. You asked what will happen if you don't wear a helmet. Look at me, this is what will happen to your children. I lost my father in a road accident because he wasn't wearing a helmet. If he had made it a habit to wear a helmet while riding a two-wheeler, he would have been alive today and I would have my father with me today, just as your children have you.'

Good citizenship is about acting in the interest of all—for the good of all. The SPC students understand that everyone must adhere to a basic system of functioning, which we call laws. And those laws are embedded in the constitutional structure of this country. The ecosystem SPC has created enables young people to bring change not only in their lives but in the life of their families and the community at large. Every human aspires for a better tomorrow. At SPC, we don't limit this aspiration to the level of desire. We don't want our students to preach, prosecute or politic. We inspire them to understand, imbibe and act.

Transform oneself to transform others. This is the fundamental principle of SPC. It is the model of transformation gifted to us by Mahatma Gandhi. He transformed himself to transform others. His life was his message. At SPC, every child and every functionary must imbibe and embody this spirit and reflect it in their behaviour. Our programmatic interventions are focused on building the capacities within every child to initiate and facilitate the process of self-transformation.

Our vision is to make India the global centre for solutions to complex problems by 2030. With our large percentage of a young population, this will be possible if we can ensure that every young person is an embodiment of a solution. If young people imbibe the value of self-transformation, then India will be a powerhouse of solutions that the world will rely on too.

Children are lighthouses. They have influence over their parents. Even small positive interventions by a child are appreciated by their parents who might say, 'My daughter told me to do this and so I am heeding her advice.' In summary, we have learnt that a changemaking child leads to the creation of a changemaking family.

Anecdotal evidence also suggests that when several changemaking-friendly parents come together, they can create a supportive ecosystem for young changemakers at the community level. There is an entity within SPC called the Guardian SPC. This is a convening of guardians and parents of SPC students. We have consistently noticed that during SPC annual summer camps, thousands of parents turn up on the school campus with grocery items and assist in setting up community kitchens. They do so because they care for their children who are participating in these camps. This is an immense aid in terms of funding and support. This year's summer camp will be the biggest so far and we expect 1,00,000 parents from the Guardian SPC community to join us in running and managing the SPC annual camp. They will also get an opportunity to interact with each other and further deepen the spirit of changemaking at the community level.

SPC has triggered a massive transformation in the police force too. The police can influence people in two ways. First, the usual method of deploying the fear factor. Through SPC, they learnt the second method: to explore and find a common ground and allow it to grow it for common good. If today's children are becoming better citizens, then the benefit will partially accrue to the police since there will be empathetic police personnel in the force, as well as law-abiding citizens.

The shift in societal perception of the police over the years because of SPC raises a couple of insightful questions. First, does the common person on the ground inherently feel that the police exist for their safety and security, especially those belonging to vulnerable sections of society—women, underprivileged folks, homeless people and children? Second, does the public trust the police?

While these two questions are important, one must also acknowledge the role that the police have played in India's internal security, without which it would be challenging to keep India united. At the same time, one can no longer ignore the changes to come in the next twenty-five years. The police have to move from being seen as a hostile force to a constructive one working towards building societal consciousness and collective action for the good of all. SPC has reimagined schools as innovation hubs across all spheres in addition to being learning centres. An ecosystem has been created to support young people to self-identify as changemakers. After all, SPC's motto is 'We learn to serve.'

2

From the Shadows to the Light

Year 2006. The town hall in the heart of Kochi had a festive look. Festoons swayed in the gentle breeze and cheerful residents milled around the venue. Police Commissioner P. Vijayan had convened a meeting of residents' associations. Children from selected schools in the city were also brought in for an informal interaction. But through the eyes of the children, he saw a different side of police. For them, the police were cruel manipulators who always sided with evil. Those were the stories they had seen, heard and believed. This propelled him to undertake an incredible journey of establishing the SPC programme.

Sixteen years later, the SPC programme is operational in 13,000 schools all over India, out of which 1,000 are from Kerala with 9,00,000 students trained so far to be compassionate, caring and conscious changemakers for the good of all. When Vijayan looks into their eyes today, he feels connected to their intense passion for an egalitarian and progressive India.

It is time for us to realise that society becomes peaceful and progressive when the number of law enforcers comes down—not when it goes up. This situation can be corrected only through conscious effort. Only then will a society be created where people respect and understand each other while celebrating differences. The idea of the SPC programme originated from the need to create a young generation that can bring about such a conscious engagement in society. The essence of the programme is to cultivate awareness among children that a democratic society should honour the laws of the people, created by the people, for the people. A generation of such empowered youth can realise the dream of a just and peaceful society, which is just a myth for us now. In fact, the SPC programme is an ongoing journey towards that goal.

Today, due to the influence of student police cadets, school students no longer fear the police. Instead, they view them as part of a supportive community. The cadets play a significant role, from being first responders during humanitarian crises to being torchbearers of duty-bound citizenship. They serve in these roles while also inspiring their peers to do the same. The change caused by the SPC programme is so profound that if today's children see the police as a comforting and reassuring presence, it is indeed the program's victory. The model, presented by Kerala, with its focus on student police cadets, is now being adopted across India.

When Vijayan took over as the Police Commissioner of Kochi, the city was reeling under a rising crime graph. He actively pursued community engagement programmes to augment efforts to enforce core policing basics through public cooperation. That is how he narrowed down on Udaya Colony, the breeding ground for criminals in Kochi. This low-income residential area was a hub for drug peddlers, muggers and snatchers, known in common parlance as goondas. He asked the sub-inspector of the Kadavanthra police station, which had jurisdiction over Udaya Colony, to organise a gathering of the residents at the community hall.

A bunch of decrepit, unkempt people gathered, many reeking of cheap country liquor and tobacco.

> From the podium, as I spoke about the need to abide by the law, I looked around, searching for a face that responded positively to what I was trying to communicate. There was none. They had seen many such attempts; nothing had happened to date. When I stepped out of the community hall, I was disappointed. I stood distraught near my official vehicle for a long time and tried to recap the experience I just had. Then my eyes caught an amazing sight.

A group of children were screaming and playing in the dirt in an open space nearby. They were unperturbed by the police commissioner's vehicle, the accompanying police jeeps or even the fact that their parents had been summoned for a gathering at the community hall. They were used to police moving around inside their colony. The sight of the children against the setting sun played in a loop in his mind for many days.

Soon, Vijayan launched Operation Candlelight to support the children of Udaya Colony in their schooling. On Christmas Day in 2005, these children presented Shakespeare's *Othello*, in English—their parents were brimming with pride. They did not understand a word, but they were all glowing in the light emanated by their children. That marked the first step for the 120-odd children from Udaya Colony to step out of the world of crime and into the bright light of mainstream society.

Vijayan was clear that his priority was to win the confidence of the public. He strengthened standard policing practices such as actionable intelligence gathering, effective day and night beat patrols, surveillance of known anti-social elements, meticulous investigation procedures and effective follow-up of prosecution. He knew this wasn't enough to instil confidence in the public. Vijayan recollects the early days in these words:

I tried an innovative concept of shadow policing. Ninety personnel from the 2,500-strong city police force were selected for their flair in crime detection, their capacities were enhanced and then deployed to crime-prone areas in civilian attires. Their objective was to blend into the crowd and prevent crime. This immediately created a sense of security among the public and fear among anti-social.

Having thus won the confidence of the public, I moved quickly to enlist their cooperation. I started organising interactions with sixty residents' associations in the city. These interactions progressed and by the time I left, there were more than 800 of them.

The idea was to prompt the citizens to come forward and organise themselves so they could better cooperate with the police. It started with monthly interactions of selected office bearers of residents' associations. An existing apex body called PRIDE, short for Police Residents Associations Interaction in District Ernakulam, was strengthened. PRIDE decided to hold a gathering of residents' associations and senior officials of the city police and civic representatives. This later evolved into the Janamaitri Initiative, a unique Kerala model of community policing.

What is interesting is that along with the first meeting held at town hall in the heart of the city, Vijayan organised an interaction with children too. While the elders gathered in the main hall on the ground floor, the smaller hall on the first floor was filled with 400 excited children selected from different schools in the city. Before the interactions got going, a blank paper was circulated amongst the children and they were asked to write about their impression of the police.

Much to Vijayan's alarm, a vast majority of the children who attended thought poorly of the police. This was even though these children hadn't had bad experiences with the police or knew of any such incident from their parents. Some of them hadn't ever interacted with a police officer until the gathering. They had developed this impression of the police force from films, media and the world around them. The mismatch in perception was quite staggering.

The public viewed the police as unfriendly, insensitive and brutal. On their part, the police considered the public as unfriendly, non-cooperative and non-law abiding. This disharmony resulted from an absence of opportunities to work together for mutual benefit.

Vijayan's reflection was this:

While the Police Academy taught me that in a democratic country, police are citizens in uniform and every citizen is a police officer without uniform, on the ground I found a huge deficit in the mutual trust between the police and citizens. I knew immediately that something must be done to correct this. Can a constructive platform for children to engage with the police result in better perception management? There was too much darkness, and I was looking for some light.

For several days, Vijayan's restless mind reminded him of his journey in life from a child worker to a police officer. In the 1970s and 1980s, the folks at Puthoormadam, an idyllic, sleepy village in Kozhikode—also known as Calicut— wouldn't have imagined that one of their own could break into the much sought-after Indian Police Service. Even Vijayan did not have the remotest idea of such a possibility. As a child, he was either in the verdant paddy fields or at a construction site as a child worker employed on daily wages. He returned home every evening, tired and drained out. But sleep was still hours away for him as he caught up with lessons from school. On Saturdays, which was payday, he would walk to the village store to buy provisions for the week. As he walked back home, he would revise the lessons learnt through the week.

So, when he joined the Indian Police Service as one of the thirty-six officers selected from across the country in 1999, he had a resolution and two clear goals in his mind. He resolved to do everything he could to ensure that children didn't suffer the harsh realities of life as he had. His two goals were, first, to become the best police officer who upheld honesty and the highest levels of professionalism to serve the cause of justice. Second, to leverage his professional position to transform the lives of children.

Before the dust settled down in front of town hall in Kochi that evening in 2006, Vijayan had learnt many lessons from his teachers—children who fearlessly engaged and shared their views with police officials. After reading the harsh comments about the police force, he planned for the children to accompany uniformed personnel to police stations—some handled traffic on the road for a while, others went along with officers for beat patrolling. At the end of these immersive visits, the children appreciated the goodness of those who donned the police uniform.

For the next two years, Vijayan developed the idea of a constructive interface between children and the law. He talked to many, discussed the idea with like-minded people and by 2008, had drafted a proposal. He shared it with Kodiyeri Balakrishnan, the then Minister for Home, Kerala. The minister immediately instructed him to submit a formal proposal and make a presentation to officials at the ministry.

The SPC programme was the result of this curious quest to reimagine schools as innovation hubs to unleash generations of informed young citizens. This is a two-year programme for high school students to inculcate citizenship responsibilities. It deeply ingrains in them the values espoused by the Constitution of India, helps them understand how law-abiding citizens contribute to societal harmony and progress for all and enhances the leadership potential in the children. Apart from inculcating respect for the law, the programme focuses on enhancing inner capabilities, self-discipline, civic sense, empathy for the vulnerable sections of society and resistance to social evils.

The transformative objective of the programme is to initiate a generational shift by creating an army of changemakers capable and willing to convert India's demographic bulge into a demographic dividend. The SPC programme has ingrained the four Cs of the twenty-first century: critical thinking, creativity, communication and collaboration. It is implemented as a collaborative programme between the departments of the state government and departments of home, education, health, forest, excise, SC/ST and social welfare and civil society at large.

As instructed by the state government, a pilot project was implemented in 2008 at Government Vocational Higher Secondary School, Iringole; St Peter's School, Kolenchery in Ernakulam district; and Government Higher Secondary School, Alappuzha. Two years later, at the Kerala School Youth Festival, the largest confluence of school students in Asia, SPC captured the imagination of government authorities and civil society. The cadets were roped in to augment the organisation of this mega-annual event in Kozhikode. The confidence with which the cadets pulled off their responsibilities won the hearts and minds of the public and the media.

After the impressive show at Kozhikode, the Government of Kerala launched the SPC project across the state in 2010. The programme was launched in 120 schools with 44 students in each batch. Even then, people were not sure what this force of children in uniform was all about. Some confused it with the NCC, others with the NSS.

Three years later, in 2013, Prime Minister Narendra Modi, who was the then Chief Minister of Gujarat, sent a delegation led by Hasmukh Patel IPS, a top Gujarat police official, to Kerala to study the programme. He spent many days with cadets, parents, teachers, SPC officials, top police officials and bureaucrats and interacted with the home minister and chief minister. He then presented a detailed report to the Government of Gujarat, which led to the launch of the SPC programme on a large scale.

Haryana and Rajasthan followed suit. Official delegations from these states travelled through Kerala to study the SPC programme in detail. Soon, these states also had student cadets proudly marching along. In 2014, K.J. George, the then Minister of Home in Karnataka, visited Kerala. Vijayan shared a detailed presentation with him and soon, Karnataka joined the list of states adopting SPC.

The next big turn in SPC history took place when the then Union Minister for Home, Rajnath Singh, visited Kerala in January 2017. He was bowled over by the show of professional discipline, enthusiasm and patriotic spirit of more than 6,000 cadets.

The very next day, he announced the possibilities of a national roll-out of the programme on social media. Ten days after his first visit, the minister returned to Kerala with a retinue of officials from the Ministry of Home Affairs. This time, he had fifteen queries ready with him. In the presence of the home secretary, state police chief and other top police officials, Vijayan made an elaborate presentation, answering all doubts the minister had raised.

Impressed with the achievements of SPC, Singh instructed the Bureau of Police Research and Development to prepare a detailed report for the national rollout. A mega event was convened in Gurugram in Haryana, where thousands of children, including thirty student police cadets, representatives from all states running the programme, participated. Singh, in the presence of Union Human Resources Development

Minister Prakash Javedkar, Haryana Chief Minister Manohar Lal Khattar and other dignitaries, rolled out SPC on a national level in July 2018. This meant that financial assistance from the union government was released for the implementation of the SPC programme.

UNICEF stepped into partnership with the SPC programme and declared student police cadets as Child Rights Ambassadors. Delegates from Tanzania, Ghana and Kazakhstan visited and there were enquiries about the programme from Sri Lanka, Maldives and many other countries. Indeed, student police cadets have started their march across the globe.

Vijayan's SPC initiative is embedded in some key strategic insights, which he discusses below:

> While designing the SPC programme, I was determined to incorporate all the feedback I received from school students whenever I interacted with them. We know that school students will become responsible citizens of tomorrow—be they politicians, bureaucrats, entrepreneurs, jurists, police personnel and so on if rightly trained and mentored. But what if this does not happen? This is critical in our times because global demographic trends show that 25.65 per cent of the global population is below the age of 14 years and 42 per cent below the age of 25 years. Among all developing nations, India is home to the world's largest youth population, with one-third of its population aged less than 14 years, half of the population aged around 25 years and 65 per cent below 35 years.

In that, India is leading the general trend among many other developing nations. While 67.2 per cent of the population is aged under 24 years in Nicaragua, youth make up 65.3 per cent of the population in Cambodia. About half of 83 million people in Vietnam are under 25 years, while 40.3 per cent of the total population in Nepal and 23 per cent in Sri Lanka are youngsters.

As Pulitzer award-winning author Thomas Friedman once said,

> The nation that will make most progress is the one that converts its young population to a demographic dividend and the nation that fails to do so will face not just the bane of unemployment, but the task of handling the unruliest crowd of young population.

Statistics by the World Health Organization (WHO) show that 14–20 per cent of children face different mental challenges. The third-biggest reason for death among youngsters is suicide. Children nowadays tend to experience extreme emotional and psychological stress and some of them are getting addicted to alcohol and drugs at a tender age. Social deviance among children is a serious risk today. Another frightening aspect is the rising tendency of children to get lured by extremist ideologies and commit violent activities. Vijayan writes:

> Unhealthy tendencies first emerge in thoughts, which lead to undesirable actions. Our actions define our way of living, peace and tranquillity in society. From religious extremism in India to neo-Nazi movements across Europe, radicalisation and extremism have targeted and succeeded in recruiting

youth. At least fifty-eight non-state armed groups in fifteen countries are recruiting and using children.

The above-mentioned trends endorse my vision regarding the success of twenty-first century policing. It largely depends on how law enforcement agencies constructively engage with children and youth and the rate of success lies in forging positive changemaking collaborations.

I am a firm believer in the fact that we all have inherent strengths. I am so sure about it because I could overcome all hurdles in my own life due to this conviction I had about myself. As the renowned English poet T.S. Eliot wrote,

> Nothing is impossible, nothing,
> To men of faith and conviction,
> Let us therefore make perfect our will.

These words always gave me the courage to pursue my passion, says Vijayan.

As motivational speaker Les Brown once noted,

The graveyard is the richest place on earth because it is here that you will find all the hopes and dreams that were never fulfilled, the books that were never written, the songs that were never sung, the inventions that were never shared, the cures that were never discovered, all because someone was too afraid to take that first step, keep with the problem, or determined to carry out their dream.

Taking forward this argument, Vijayan says,

This is most often caused by the absence of a conscious effort to train oneself. Only those who have identified their talents and nurtured it move ahead and make a mark on life. We need to make this investment in children for impressive results. If we can influence the children creatively before conceptual and intellectual debris pollutes their minds, we can create magic using their innovative thoughts and incessant energy. However, their talents cannot be creatively engaged only through inspiration and shallow awareness campaigns, it takes a systematic and scientifically designed training regime to fine-tune the talents of children.

Another quality that we need to ingrain in our children is to make democracy a way of life, as India upholds a democracy anchored to the Constitution. The basic values of our Constitution, namely equality, freedom, brotherhood, secularism, democracy, unity and inclusiveness, need to be made part of their character from an early age. Also, they should be taught that the rights of a citizen arise out of their responsibilities.

Unfortunately, the bane of a nation like India is that the public is more enthusiastic about breaking the law than following it. Blatant violations of law occur on our roads and other public spaces every day. The core efficiency of a vibrant democratic society is the law made by the public for the public. In other words, the public in a nation should own up to the rule of law. Children should grow up with the true conviction that the rule of the law in their nation is designed to ensure their freedom and security. Instead of insulting the law or being afraid of it, our children should be proud of it and feel that upholding the law is their own responsibility.

Civic sense is the stamp of all developed societies. Behaviour such as ignoring the law, showing disrespect to the rights of others, callous attitude towards the environment and irresponsible, unsustainable ways of living, like dumping garbage on the streets, should raise concern. The lasting solution to this is inculcating a civic sense in our children right from an early age.

The contribution of responsible citizens towards nation-building will be effective only if divisive ideas are abandoned, and all are focused on the collective progress of the nation. Any thoughts on caste, religion, language, creed or community should come only after the concern for the nation as one entity. The idea of India and the Constitution should supersede any other faith or ideology. Our children should feel proud of the rich heritage of our land. According to Vijayan,

> This can be achieved only by building a society that keeps the feeling of India in their words, deeds and thoughts; a society that is committed to upholding the dignity of the nation by abiding by the law and keeping healthy mind and body at work to fight back against all social evils and most importantly, a society that transforms and values everyone as a change leader. The Student Police Cadet project is designed to meet these goals. It has not been inspired by any other similar interventional social organisation but has evolved into an agency of its own as a response to the general environment. That makes the SPC project firmly rooted in its milieu and has the immense potential of integrating the possibilities of modern times.

This vision is clearly outlined in the ten declarations of the SPC programme:

1. I respectfully abide by the laws of the land.
2. I respect the rights of others and will do my utmost to uphold them.

3. I strive to improve my physical and mental fitness and refrain from activities that are detrimental to my health and well-being.
4. We cannot exist without our environment. I am committed to the protection of our earth, air and water.
5. I love my fellow beings. I will overcome any adversity and help those in need.
6. I am open-minded and celebrate diversity.
7. I am a patriot with a global outlook. I love my country and fellow citizens irrespective of any caste, religion, gender, ethnicity and language differences.
8. Democracy is my culture. I am aware of my own rights and my duties towards others.
9. I am aware of the challenges and opportunities of the twenty-first century and am committed to lead the realisation of Sustainable Development Goals (SDGs).
10. I am a change leader. I strive to realise my potential, spread the message of goodness and lead by example for social change.

When he began his career with the Indian Police Service, Vijayan's mind had been filled with doubts about the extent to which the police could intervene to bring about social changes. Now, after fifteen years of trial and error, corrections and revisions, the SPC programme is living proof that the police can be at the forefront of bringing about positive social change. The COVID-19 pandemic and the 2018 Kerala floods demonstrated that student police cadets can indeed rise to the challenge and uphold their motto. From 2008 to

2023, the programme underwent many catalytic moments, withstanding challenges by raising the bar.

The path to the future is clear for every trained student police cadet. Each of these cadets, disciplined, ethically upright, compassionate, courageous and caring, will be an asset to India. The SPC community has made it a life mission to help create a better tomorrow for everyone.

3

Reimagining Schools as Changemaking Hubs

Schools in Kerala can broadly be classified into three types: government, government-aided and private schools. Government schools are run completely by the state government and follow the state syllabus in Malayalam, which is the native language of Kerala. English-medium sections are possible within such schools; however, it is subject to the fulfilment of specific conditions laid down by the government.

Government-aided schools can be Malayalam or English medium. They are owned and managed by non-governmental or private agencies and religious organisations and follow the state syllabus. The government pays the salary of its teaching and non-teaching staff in order to facilitate subsidised education for students.

The third category of private, unaided schools operates almost exclusively in English medium and are privately owned and managed. These schools charge a fee and are mostly affiliated to the Indian Council of Secondary Education (ICSE), the Central Board of Secondary Education (CBSE) or the Indian Secondary Education (ISE) education boards. In Kerala, approximately 36 per cent of all schools are government schools, 57 per cent are aided schools and 7 per cent are private schools.

When it comes to the implementation of the SPC program, the primary targets are government and government-aided schools. For formal consideration to join the SPC program, a school needs to apply through the office of the local Circle Inspector (CI). Interestingly, the SPC administration tends to favour schools that lack any youth development initiatives, seeing an opportunity to fill this gap with the SPC programme.

However, the introduction of 'grace marks' in 2012—extra academic points awarded for participation in extracurricular activities like SPC—led to increased competition among schools to adopt the program. As noted by one Assistant District Nodal Officer (ADNO), this concept of 'grace marks' significantly increased interest in the SPC programme compared to its initiation in 2010.

Importantly, implementing the SPC programme in reputable schools was also beneficial for enhancing the image and reputation of the SPC. This established a mutually beneficial relationship where schools could gain prestige and academic benefits from associating with the SPC, while the programme itself expanded its societal reach and recognition. As such, the SPC programme began to proliferate in popular schools, boosting their growth in tandem with its own

Three distinct and equally important parts make up a school: staff, students and parents (or the community at large). All of these components are involved in the functioning and thriving of the school; these apply to SPC schools as well.

Let us first take a look at the staff and understand how SPC has made an impact on them. We have fantastic examples in this book of the varied, effective and innovative projects done by SPC in different schools. The role community police officers (CPOs) play in conceptualising, implementing and maintaining these projects is significant. That said, the sheer number of projects done under the SPC banner in different parts of the state is incredible and, in a way, shows the commitment the school ecosystem has towards the programme. Into this ecosystem, the police, through SPC, lend a sense of authority and legitimacy to their creative enterprise. This is possible because schools are now hubs for extraordinary innovation and have begun to step outside the comfort zone of imparting education, all thanks to the contributions made by student police cadets. Schools are encouraging and supporting cadets in identifying and working for social causes.

One of the best things about SPC has been the creation of a nebulous space that allows for continuous innovation to occur. This space wasn't part of the original design but was created unintentionally and grew on its own when commitment and intent from drill instructors (DIs) and CPOs met the creativity and enthusiasm of the SPC. Once the concept of schools as innovation hubs took hold, the government supported and encouraged this diversification and the school ecosystem became a learning community, experimenting and innovating to drive SPC forward. It is a testament to the leadership of

SPC that enabled teachers, police personnel and students to push the boundaries of regular schooling and innovate new means of making a difference to society and schools.

As of now, teachers, students, parents and other community members are converging in schools and that nebulous space is where a lot of action is taking place—a place where everyone gains something. At the end of the day, SPC has created—or at least reimagined and repositioned—schools as social innovation hubs. Consequently, SPC has also has sharpened the edge of community policing. When school children aspire to create a plastic-free locality and their initiative is backed by the local police station as a social intervention, the authenticity of this intervention is seen as legitimatised by the state, even if in an informal way. Even if it is just a bunch of SPC school kids stepping out to do something, the community is aware that the police support the initiative. There is an invisible cloak of authority, authenticity and trust, and because kids are implementing it, the intervention is legitimate and prolonged.

Let's take the example of a school that is working on reducing plastic use in its panchayat. This came about in a seemingly innocuous way when, for World Environment Day 2014, CPO Nandini of a government school in Pattikad, Thrissur, encouraged her group of cadets to use a part of the school grounds to grow vegetables that could be sold to support malnourished children from a certain community. Teeshma Abraham, a young cadet, was dismayed to find a large amount of buried plastic waste when the students dug a hole to plant a sapling. This prompted the children to clean up their school and free it from plastic waste. This movement seeped into the homes of the children and then spread across the entire community. Soon enough, others joined in on the action. By that time, the children had moved on to clear an area by the local dam and in the process helped save some flora that was specific to that locality and was otherwise endangered by the polluted land. The Mukti programme continues and has garnered momentum over the years since its inception. If it had not been for the resourcefulness of the children and the dogged pursuit of their goal to rid their community of dangerous plastic waste, these endangered herbs may have vanished into the night without a trace.

Another example of a meaningful SPC project took place in an untouched corner of Palakkad. Student cadets physically carried a voting machine into a remote community to educate and encourage members of the Kurumba tribe, making them one of the earliest users of AutoPay in the district that had never participated in elections. Not only did these children—some of whom belonged to the same community—teach the villagers how to use the machine, they also educated them on their civic responsibility of voting and participating in the electoral process. Rajeswari M., a Grade X student of Government Vocational Higher Secondary School (GVHSS) Agali in Palakkad, was a police cadet from a marginalised community who stepped up to answer the concerns of the tribal women in their mother tongue when they put the team in a spot with questions about the rationale for their involvement in the election when nobody bothered to take care of them afterwards.

What could have been an embarrassing encounter was quickly converted into an empowering dialogue, both for the women and the cadets. What is more laudable is the commitment Rajeswari and others showed by returning to the community *after* the elections to consolidate and take the questions, requests and difficulties of the inhabitants to the authorities. Her sense of responsibility shines through in the intent she voiced: 'We will go back to them, get their complaints, and demands noted and forward it to the authorities. That was a promise we made to them, and we will fulfil it.' This is another beautiful example of how SPC projects empower and build leadership capabilities and a sense of responsibility in their cadets. It is a powerful testament to the commitment and tenacity of the SPC team in taking the community from 0 per cent poll participation to a 100, as their intervention led all twenty members to cast their votes.

Some SPC schools are lucky to have highly imaginative, enthusiastic CPOs and DIs, not to mention nodal officers-in-charge. The sheer numbers of projects these schools are able to conceive and float is phenomenal. For instance, cadets run a radio club from a specially designed audio booth inside a school where a few years ago, twenty-five radio jockeys were trained. These young professionals now have ten minutes on air at 1.30 p.m. on fixed days of the week. They share news, songs and stories.

A skill hub established for eighty-eight cadets in a school brings out an entire spectrum of products from utility bags made out of newspaper to homemade cakes for Christmas. Some of the cadets are actively engaged in LED lamp assembling units, while others handle the budding of saplings. The skill hub ensures that students are adept in at least two skills by the time they complete the course and pass out of school. So, in addition to improving their personality and civic sense, there is also the willingness to get down and dirty to get work done and truly understand the dignity of labour.

The search for new and innovative concepts keeps teachers and students thinking on their toes and finding out-of-the-box solutions to existing problems—some of which may not have been recognised as 'problems' in the past. A good example of this is the medicinal garden that was planted and maintained by cadets. Here, approximately eighty plants are grown with support from the Jawaharlal Nehru Tropical Botanical Garden and Research Institute (TBGRI), a premier institution in research and conservation biology. The children did a wonderful job using modern technology to bring changes into the cataloguing system of this enterprise; they prepared a QR-code-based recognition and information system for every plant in the garden.

Many CPOs even pay for the projects out of their own pockets after completely using up the basic budget the SPC board provides them, but they are admittedly happy to do so; the sense of accomplishment they get from the success of the projects, the pride and confidence this fosters in their cadets and the effect on the community is sometimes considered payment enough.

Here is a thought worth considering: how many policemen do you think might take teenage school children directly into muddy paddy fields to experience farming in all its majesty?

DI Nizarudeen of Vithura Police Station Thiruvananthapuram provided a part of his family's paddy field to allow children the unadulterated experience of farming. This came about after his interactions with cadets in Vithura, when he realised that the students had no idea what a haystack was. For someone who came from an agrarian family, this was a confounding experience that got him thinking about what he could do to help the children gain first-hand knowledge of agriculture and farming, in addition to their core subjects at school. With this idea in mind, he talked to his uncle who had cultivable paddy fields and arranged for the students to take up cultivation in a field spanning half an acre.

Take the case of CPO Anver of Vithura. After DI Nizarudeen's initiative of bringing paddy farming home to the students was a great success, he helped expand their reach to aqua-farming. CPO Anver came up with the Bhaksya Suraksha, Manava Raksha (Secure Food, Save Humanity) project. The project itself had four separate components, the first being farming paddy and fish alternatively in paddy fields, which would result in nutrients being replenished into the field with fish farming after they were absorbed by the paddy crop. The second component involved planting and maintaining coconut trees of a dwarf variety. The third component was a zero-budget spiritual farming concept wherein grow bags with natural manure like the dung of indigenous cows were used for micro-farming. The fourth and final component was a heritage garden that only had indigenous tubers. This project was instrumental in teaching the youth to find inspired and inspirational innovations outside academics.

Within the SPC, students are also trained to rise above identity markers such as caste, religion and language as these only lead to unnecessary conflict and provoke students to engage in destructive behaviour. Rather, students are expected to repose their faith in social and political institutions that work for the improvement of civic life and, among other things, assist the police in maintaining peace by providing information about criminals and criminal activities. Take the case of police cadet Surya KC of Girls' Higher Secondary School (GHSS), Thalappuzha in Wayanad. Surya belonged to the Kurichiyar tribe, located within Makkimala in the forests of Kerala. Despite their reclusive lives inside the forest with a preference for minimal interaction with outsiders, the Kurichiyars were often approached by activist groups encouraging them to revolt against the state and the police force that sought to suppress these activists. And although the community preferred to live out their lives quietly within their community and stay out of the mainstream, as a people, they were caught between the police force and the activists, who were both outsiders. The training and exposure Surya received as a police cadet led her to notice things and question the activists—the latter being an unheard-of quality in her tribe. To cut a long story short, she identified a couple of visitors to her hamlet as activists in the wanted list circulated by the police and the clear information she provided led to their arrest.

One would imagine a child from her neck of the woods—quite literal in this particular case since they did stay inside the remote recesses of a forest—would be satisfied with the arrest and not want to do more. However, Surya decided she would also testify against the outsiders in court, thereby defying an age-old custom of her people that had them stay within their hamlet. That said, once she graduated from SPC, despite having shown such incredible, unflinching initiative and resolve, she reverted to being the typical Kurichiyar maiden. As with all girls in the community, she was married off really young. She may have harboured certain dreams at some point in her young life owing to her connection with SPC and the opportunities it presented; however, after graduating from the system, she was constrained to live her life within the traditional boundaries set for her.

This leads to some really poignant questions. Is there something more SPC—or the force behind SPC—can do to ensure the continued development of the empowered youth? How can we get the community more involved to showcase the greatness of cadets? What more can be done for the cadets who graduate from the programme and move on with their respective lives? What is the point in awakening leadership capabilities in a person if, after graduation from the programme, there is no way to ensure their progress in pursuing and realising their hopes and dreams?

It's clear that while there have been incredible projects because of the SPC programmes, certain concerns need to be ironed out. One of the concerns being raised is that the emphasis has been more on numbers than quality. Who is measuring the quality of the projects and what really gets done? While some SPC schools have worked on an overwhelming number of award-winning projects, others haven't brought out as many and have little to show for their efforts. Another issue is the paucity of funds. Many projects require deep pockets, which means schools have to find other means of supporting these activities and the officials who engage with them.

Another concern is the friction between the teachers and the police. In the early days, CPOs—especially women— expressed very often that their role as teachers was not acknowledged within the SPC. Even though they contributed significantly, the credit was being taken solely by the police. There was a sense of resentment that their identity as teachers was being marginalised. If the CPO had a great relationship with the local SPC-designated police officer, then it would go well, but the opposite was true as well. There was a time when teachers insisted that they wanted the SPC Teachers Association to look into their grievances. But it only helped to slightly normalise the image of the police and actually help them.

In Kerala society, teachers are a highly respected authoritative intellectual class, while the police are normally seen beating up people. A lot of the imagery of the Kerala police is connected with violence and not really in sync with society. So, when teachers wore police uniforms, it was not an unproblematic taking up of authority or prestige; police constables are very sensitive to this power. The teachers' respect in society didn't go down; however, they were keenly aware that while contributing towards legitimising the SPC's role in the school, their authority was not clear even though they were designated as CPO with a sub-inspector (SI) rank. For instance, when, in the initial days of training, CPOs in uniform were first honoured and then talked down by regular police constables, it created a lot of embarrassment for the teachers.

Babu, who held the position of assistant state nodal officer, talked about the 'perceived injustice' of the CPO being 'given' the honorary rank of SI and a uniform with two stars while it took eleven years of service for regular police personnel to earn it. According to him, the constable with eight years of service may not want to salute a CPO who is not even 'regular' police, and the only difference in uniform is the letters indicating Kerala Police or SPC Project. It was natural for the lower-ranked police person to salute the teacher wearing the officers' uniform and then regret it when they realise a salute had been 'wasted' on the 'undeserving'. In his opinion, it was not just the teachers who had trouble with the police officer uniforms, it was also the police personnel who went through training and years of experience in the force who felt let down.

Wearing the uniform was a matter of pride, but it was also a contested field that resulted in them wearing uniforms only during drill days. Unsaid social contracts have also developed between the teachers and cops, which is why the police never enforce the uniform for teachers. Close association with the police either created a lot of resentment in the teachers that only a few teachers were selectively accepted or 'built up' within SPC. The others felt they were doing the work but not given the status, so much so that the resentment resulted in the chosen few teachers being isolated and not even invited to some 'special' meetings.

In the case of the police force, CPOs and ACPOs are encouraged or discouraged based on the attitude of the principals of the school. This makes a huge difference in the quality of projects and the work the particular school does with SPC. In schools, just like in police stations, some principals were sensitive to the role the CPO played. However, there were also many principals who considered SPC a distraction with few perks. In such cases, the CPOs were overloaded with work that made it practically impossible for them to function productively in both roles. Many gave up and sought transfers to lesser-known schools that didn't have SPC just to stop the 'persecution'. Also, in the course of discussions, we came across a few teachers who chose to relinquish their roles in SPC because it was too stressful. Going forward, SPC has to be really careful about the inevitability of some teachers outshining others and be sensitive and pragmatic in dealing with how teachers are acknowledged within the system.

The teachers and the school ecosystem have played a big role in legitimising and creating space for police to intervene in social issues. Some of the police officers were interested in reiterating the role they played in creating this opportunity for kids. They discussed how SPC brought discipline into the school system—a narrative that often offended teachers because they believed, quite rightly, that there existed a form of discipline in schools even before the SPC. The DI and CPO are both equally important and form the foundation of SPC, with support from the community and schools as innovation hubs, but that seems to be a relationship that has not been looked into enough.

It is not difficult to understand where we may have missed the bus on this so far since the SPC directorate works within the police headquarters and is staffed by police; it is only natural that they will look at it through a different lens. This 'connection' has also been of tremendous help to CPOs on many occasions. Take the case of CPO Sreeja from Erumappetty in Thrissur. When one of her SPC cadets came to her, concerned about a voyeur videotaping her taking a bath during the days leading up to the Republic Day parade for which they had congregated in an area outside of their homes, the teacher directly got in touch with the Commissioner of

Police and resolved the issue quickly and effectively. According to Sreeja, such a response would not have been possible without her involvement with SPC.

All of this said, many powerful stories have remained private within SPC. One such story involves a cadet who strove towards her goal at SPC despite having lost her entire family. As a young girl, she lost her mother when her sibling was born; the event deeply affected her as it would any child her age and also scarred her father severely. As time went on, she turned herself into a surrogate mother to her little sister and life moved forward. Eventually, her father remarried and the family expanded, but the girls remained bonded with the elder one playing mother and the younger one stepping in as her loudest and staunchest cheerleader.

At some point in time, the guilt and thoughtless remarks from friends and relatives started preying on the father's mind, and he began imbibing alcohol freely, getting abusive and violent. One day, he lost it completely and tried to harm the girls. The young cadet managed to save herself. But the father took the life of her sister and then killed himself, leaving her destitute and despondent. The piteous cries of her little sister rang in her ears and almost drove her mad with guilt and grief, but in her own words, thanks to her training and the support she received from SPC, she could recover from the pain of the experience and build bridges. She now has a renewed positive relationship with her stepmother and looks at everything that happened in her childhood through a new lens, intent on continuing her education and making a difference in this world. Stories such as hers deserve to be told.

4

A Humane Police
How SPC Transformed Kerala Police

One of the unintended consequences of SPC has been the refreshing image makeover of the Kerala police. The police are professionally trained to strictly treat violations of law as offences. With the advent of SPC, the interactions between police and students acquired the depth of a mentor–mentee relationship. That said, it was the authority of the police that made SPC so attractive for schools to adopt and for families to see their children in uniform.

The impression of authority, efficiency, discipline and power associated with wearing the uniform is an important ingredient of the attractiveness of SPC in Kerala. Student cadets are seen as 'kutty police' or child police. For a long time within policing circles, conversations on SPC usually focused only on how the programme enhanced discipline in schools. Now, there is open acknowledgement of how SPC has helped make the police more socially conscious and compassionate.

In her doctoral thesis, Dr Ann Mary Chacko discusses how the word 'police' generated a sense of fear. With time, the sight of students wearing the uniform and the whole school community, including parents, interacting closely with the police, the fear decreased. As such, while there's no doubt the authority of the police made SPC attractive to schools, it's also undeniable that the cadets aided in improving public opinion of the police in Kerala.

Chacko points out,

> Contrast this with, for instance, the police–school interactions in the US, which is a much more criminalising kind of interaction. In the US, the police are stationed within schools. In New York City, NYPD has stations within schools and one of the consequences of this is that even routine discipline issues get criminalised.

In this context, it is noteworthy to notice the humane interaction between police and schools in Kerala.

Chacko continues.

> I was completely taken aback by my observations of the humane interaction between police and schools. I was not seeing the police as a dystopia. And in fact, I received pushback from my own dissertation committee, saying that you seem to have gone native, like in anthropology there is this concept of going native, where you kind of identify yourself too much with the community you're studying. They asked me, 'What are you missing? After all, the police are a force of violence. It is the violent arm of the state.'

Fifteen years ago, it would have been impossible to predict that the Kerala police would gain the confidence of hundreds of thousands of youngsters and their parents. A glowing testament to the above is the zero-budget short film *Killing Smoke* that a Class VIII student from Bhavan's Vidya Mandir, Eroor, Sreehari Rajesh, made by pulling together some of his friends and police personnel. In Sreehari's words, the movie ends with 'the police coming to know about his drug use and taking him to a better life through counselling.' This effort left such a deep impression on Vijayan that he directed all SPC units across the state to screen the movie.

When a school student comes up with such an idea for a project, it shows the place the police have in his and his peers' minds. A group of police personnel turning up in an area would have once caused a major upheaval, but now, police escorts or police vans enter school compounds unhindered, and there is not even the slightest ripple of unease.

After Sreehari came up with the idea of the short film, he discussed it with police officers associated with SPC and with their blessings and support, he shot the movie. Some of those personnel and his friends are actors in the film as well—what a change from the dynamics of fear the police roused before SPC!

The same phenomenon of seeing the police as mentors and confidantes was also seen in other states of India where SPC was introduced. In the Andaman and Nicobar Islands, a school police cadet observed something suspicious in a marketplace, and he stealthily followed those involved. Once he realised that they were part of a group making and selling illicit liquor, he went to meet the DI at the police station to share information. The culprits were quickly arrested and the operation was shut down because of the bravery and presence of mind of the young cadet and his implicit faith in his DI.

The name of the cadet has been withheld to protect his identity but the story shows how the psychological and social barriers to open communication between students or teachers and police have broken down through SPC. Today, inviting a chief guest from the police to preside over a government school event is a matter of pride. At these events, cops do not directly talk about law enforcement; rather, they come as educators and mentors, leading the way to a highly transformative experience for both parties.

Their stories were mainly about children who were caught doing the wrong thing like watching pornography or drug use and peddling. As an official put it:

> Recently, I had been to a wedding in the family. There, I saw my relative's son, an eighth grader, with a mobile phone. I called the parent and asked him if it was necessary to give mobile phones to an eighth grader. But the parents saw no wrong in it. Then, about a month ago, the father called me up and told me that his son was in [the] police station. This child had downloaded pornographic pictures from the net, and not only that, was also sharing them with his friends. Very often these days, even parents are not aware of the kinds of activities their children are involved in.

This is an example of legitimate stories the police would bring up in conversation with criminally at-risk children and, at the same time, by using these in their narratives, young children who had fallen into the 'wrong' path gave traction for SPC's changemaking initiatives. If we really looked deep within, the unique simultaneity was that the stories of deviancy gave legitimacy to the programme aimed at creating model children. Those who were considering or had taken a wrong turn or a step in the wrong direction, when faced with such experiences, would have the opportunity to reconsider their options and maybe even reach out for help.

Some of the policemen who are directly involved with SPC have openly remarked about how this project has made them more humane. Previously, the police would employ brutal techniques of crime-solving and containment. In December 2021, Justice Devan Ramachandran, High Court of Kerala, remarked that 'this kind of conduct occurred in eighteenth-century dungeons' while reviewing a case of the police chaining a complainant to the railing and then adding insult to injury by slapping charges of obstructing a police officer from discharging his duties on the same complainant.

Such incidents, though rare, receive a great deal of publicity in the media, cementing the impression of police brutality in the minds of the public. This then makes it extremely difficult for a lay person to consider the feasibility of the police mentoring and guiding students. As the journey of SPC and those associated with it unfolds in these pages, we will be able to see quite clearly that all three categories of people associated with the project—the police, the students and the teachers—all gain from the experience as much as (if not more than) what they contribute to it; this is a case of the whole being more than the sum of its parts.

Initially at least, much before the impact of the programme was understood, the police assigned to SPC were in it for just routine chain-of-command orders. Many of the assigned police personnel were chosen and posted as DIs in SPC in addition to their regular duties and may even have viewed

SPC as 'extra duty' or an added pressure for them. In many cases, they were seen as slackers by their peers or as people who were getting away with easy duty.

In many cases, the designated DIs were given the responsibility of SPC over and above their regular roles and while some resented the additional work, others were proactive in going out of their way to make a change within the school. They took up the role of a teacher, and many even provided sports coaching to the students. Basheer, the DI of Payyampally St. Catherine's School in Mananthavady in 2015, was an artistically minded policeman who took an active part in training students in music and dance for their annual day celebrations, much like a teacher might have done.

As mentioned previously, during the earliest phase of SPC, all police personnel involved in doing SPC work were seen as slackers because of the predominant idea that 'real' police work is about extending and enforcing authority and, in most cases, involved threats and use of violence. The idea and the impression—at least in those days among the public—was that people should fear the police irrespective of whether they respect them. Constables from the lowest rung of the police force were chosen as DIs. They were the ones that never received any respect within the force. However, the experiences of older police constables who were often insulted and talked down to in public by younger, higher-ranking police officers were completely transformed after their involvement in the SPC programme. With this new responsibility, they were receiving immense respect from children and their families. Consequently, this opportunity became very transformative. Retired ASNO Babu became a trainer through the SPC programme—something he had never imagined doing until he started.

During this time, the SPC also acquired political legitimacy. Very senior cops simply picked up their phones and called the officer-in-charge of SPC directly, bypassing other higher-ranking officials in the station. And in some functions, the SPC was invited and represented and that started legitimising it in the eyes of the police. Babu fondly remembers being invited to a personal celebration at the residence of a top police officer associated with SPC.

'Had it not been for my involvement in SPC, there would have been no way I would have been there as a guest, much less after my retirement from service … In fact, my retirement function was attended by the Chief of Kerala Police—that is only because I was part of the SPC team; otherwise, he would not have had direct interactions with me,' Babu says gratefully.

Instances such as these cause subtle shifts in the balance within the force, with the 'downtrodden' officers suddenly finding themselves in the enviable position of interacting directly with high-ranking officials while being asked about their work in the schools.

This was when the other 'better' cops suddenly realised that they didn't have the status or connections that the DIs from SPC enjoyed. This changed the dynamics within the force. It was at this juncture that Kerala police personnel began realising that SPC isn't a community policing initiative. Such an initiative is about involving members of the community to reduce smuggling, alcoholism, robberies, communal tension, alcoholism-related boundary disputes—land and property disputes that occur after one party is drunk—and family fights. The police force and the policymakers took notice of the societal leadership roles that SPC was knitting within communities. This process set the base for an entirely new concept of social policing.

This period marked a turning point within the police force when officers noticed the unique status and connections that the DIs from the SPC programme enjoyed, a realisation that shifted internal dynamics. It was at this juncture that Kerala police personnel started distinguishing SPC from traditional community policing initiatives.

Community policing typically involves cooperation between the police and community members to tackle issues like smuggling, alcoholism, robberies, communal tensions and family disputes. While important, this approach mainly addresses existing societal problems.

On the other hand, the SPC began to pioneer a different approach, that is through social policing. Policymakers and the police force began to recognise how SPC was fostering societal leadership within communities. Unlike community policing, social policing through the SPC didn't merely react to societal problems. Instead, it proactively engaged young people to cultivate responsible citizenship and societal harmony, thus preventing potential issues. This transformative process laid the foundation for an entirely new concept of social policing, where the focus shifts from merely responding to issues to preventing them through the active involvement of younger generations.

The role of DIs was mainly to instil a sense of discipline among the students and pride for the uniform as well as help with general training and practice for parades. Additionally, many even helped with other skills like music, dance and sports. Many DIs went beyond the call of duty, intuitively trying their hand at teaching and getting to know the students, watching sports with them and mentoring them in different activities.

Slowly and steadily, acceptance and popularity of DIs grew in the community, and others in the police station realised that those they had considered slackers were the ones getting more respect and positive visibility among senior officers and the community at large. This was something that had not been anticipated, but the network of social capital and connections with other constables and senior officers that DIs earned through SPC meant a lot to them and encouraged them to outperform themselves, resulting in a positive cycle of involvement, performance and recognition. The sense of oneness, respect and credibility the DIs earned brought about a change in their own behaviour, and their commitment to the children affected society at large, which resulted in social capital all around.

Another positive outcome is the manner in which SPC normalised the conversation on narcotics and drugs in schools—a very difficult issue. For instance, in some schools, kids were both peddlers and consumers. Most school principals, teachers and others admitted that having an honest, transparent conversation on consumption of drugs in school is simple enough but keeping the perimeter secure is not. Cops, however, can ensure that. CPOs who delve into this highly sensitive and 'dangerous' topic do so under the condition of anonymity. According to them, students are often waylaid by antisocial elements on their way to school. At times, even auto-rickshaw drivers first offer free dope, then peddle to them and soon enough insist that the 'hooked' students either peddle drugs or bring in more 'candidates to the business'. Even when teachers come to know of such interactions, it is practically impossible for them to contain or prevent the same from happening because they have no authority outside the school premises. It is possible that this is handled more easily by the cops. CPOs were happy to state that the response from cops associated with SPC is swift when informed of such activities.

The SPC leadership is actively involved in educating students on the terrible aspects of drug use. CPOs are happy to report that cops engage in simple, mildly confrontational conversations with the students in person. They may ask questions like, 'Son, how are you doing? Are you still consuming? According to CPOs, a united front of teachers and police helps contain the menace of drug abuse in schools to a large extent. Cops typically engage in conversations in terms of cause and effect like 'if you do this, this will happen; and if you do not, that will not either.' In a way, the SPC has allowed the police to take their experience with wrongdoers and make use of it to guide others onto the right path. So, some good comes of the bad they deal with as a routine part of their job.

As discussed previously, the integrated programme crafted by the police in collaboration with fourteen government departments exemplifies a concerted effort by the Kerala government, wherein resources are deployed for the betterment of the community in general and the physical, mental and educational development of youth in particular. This school-based cadet programme seeks to strengthen the Indian democracy by shaping young minds to be responsible citizens rather than merely abiding by 'compulsory obedience.' SPC cadets are required to do around fourteen activities annually as part of this collaboration. Records show that cadets and CPOs together far exceed this number.

℺

Today, nobody can ignore the SPC programme because it enjoys political support. In 2021, when the world was in the grips of the pandemic, SPC kept growing. Virtually inaugurating the extension of SPC to 165 more schools in the state, Chief Minister Pinarayi Vijayan lauded the contributions of the programme to cultural and educational sectors.

However, this acceptance and applause from seniors and political circles created some problems for DIs within the force. An official who spoke to us on condition of anonymity mentioned that during the early days of SPC, there were instances when seniors and station writers insisted on assigning them tough duties or the graveyard shift the night before the SPC parade day. These actions can be considered retaliatory, although it should be noted that most stations did not have the manpower required to ensure that DIs, no matter what the workload of SPC, could be excused from duties in the station roster without adding to the load of the others.

A CI is in-charge of a police circle consisting of several police stations, each of which could be given charge of one or more SPC schools for which they served as the Student Police Liaison Officer (SPLO). This naturally added to the workload of CIs. All these created stress for the DI and other police personnel associated with SPC but most of them chose to keep on working with SPC because of the sense of accomplishment it gave them with respect to shaping and mentoring the cadets. Sensible suggestions from DIs included that when a station is given charge of different SPC schools, care should be taken to ensure sufficient manpower in that station.

Kerala police vans have been colloquially referred to as *idi vandi*, loosely translated to mean 'punching vehicle' referring to the punches and beatings sustained by 'suspects' who had the misfortune of being picked up and transported by the police in these vehicles. Now, many DIs have fond memories of travelling in these same vehicles with student police cadets to and from SPC conventions. Chacko discusses a trip she took in one of the *idi vandis* with cadets and police constables in preparation for the Independence Day celebrations organised by the district-level government administration.

She says,

> The cadets who were in a festive mood on our way to the parade entertained themselves by singing the latest Hindi and Malayalam film songs. It was hilarious to watch the confused and curious glances that came our way from people in adjacent vehicles when the *idi vandi* stopped at traffic lights. While cries of pain emanating from an *idi vandi* might have been a normal sight [in the past], here was an *idi vandi* filled with young girls singing with abandon!

An officer who asked to remain anonymous talked of a colleague who would routinely hit the bottle and get very abusive towards family members, especially his spouse. After he was assigned to SPC for mentoring young students, this policeman transformed himself by overcoming alcoholism and saving his marriage from the verge of total collapse. According to him, many policemen, after being assigned as DIs, gave up smoking because they felt like it brought them down in the eyes of the cadets they were mentoring and counselling against substance abuse.

Ajith, a former ASNO of SPC, has a moving story of personal transformation. In 2019, he was nominated by the government to join the Kalinga Fellowship in Delhi along with a group of students and teachers. Kalinga Fellowship is a multi-sector programme that brings together people from the government, private sector and civil society to find actionable solutions for addressing gender-based violence and human trafficking. He was close to superannuation and he thought that this might be a good way to bring an end to his long career. In Delhi, as part of the fellowship, he found himself in a team working in brothel in Delhi. For him, it was a transformative experience because as a police officer, he had been trained to look at sex workers as criminals and not as victims of trafficking.

Hitherto, his first lens was that of a police officer and for that reason, he was very uncomfortable sitting in a brothel conversing with sex workers, the brothel owner and pimps. In any other circumstance, he would have done something to enforce the law instead of sitting there and sipping tea as a quiet listener. It was difficult for him to think beyond his ideas of 'purity' and 'impurity'. A female sex worker was talking about her life when she mentioned that she was trafficked by her relatives into commercial sex work at the age of thirteen. When asked why she was not doing anything about it, she said, 'There is no point trying to get any justice from anywhere.' She said that the local policeman, whom she would have to request for help, groped and insulted her in public. The doctor at the primary health centre—who should have been the one to give her medical aid—refused to touch her. That's the mindset people have about prostitutes, she said.

For her, this was her vocation, her body was her factory through which she generated income and all she wanted was for people to accept her as she was. Ajith, who had been sitting quietly, listening to her talk, said later, 'Why did I have this experience now when I am about to retire from this office in just six months? I'm now looking at this in a completely new light.' He had tears in his eyes when he spoke—that was how moved he was by that one experience. This is a prime example of how the SPC project makes a difference in the lives, experiences and mindsets of the policemen involved.

It is important to note here that one of the reasons SPC has grown as an institution is because it listens to voices on the ground—cadets, their parents, CPOs and police personnel. As such, feedback is part of the collective effort to keep improving, deepening and enhancing the impact of the programme on the ground. That said, being a uniformed force, it still stands to reason that while retired personnel are more likely to speak up with respect to perceived indifferences or inequalities, those currently serving are more likely to limit themselves to putting up suggestions for improvement of the project.

When all is said and done, there are advantages DIs associated with SPC enjoy even after superannuation from service. Some of them have continued to be associated with SPC purely for the emotional returns it gives them, be it acceptance and respect from the community or the sense of fulfilment in doing something worthwhile over and above the duties assigned to them as part of their career.

Those who choose to pour in their creativity, sensitivity and commitment to the assignment are richly rewarded. Retired ASNO Babu is quite convinced, rightly so, of the fact that it was his association with SPC that set him apart from the run-of-the-mill constabulary, allowing him visibility in the eyes of the senior officers in an otherwise hierarchical organisation that demands respects discipline and protocol. Yet another benefit Babu is quick to point out is the acceptance in the community they enjoy as compared to other retired police personnel. He also mentions how, historically, Kerala police personnel were kept at arm's length by society at large whether or not they were in service. They did not have much of a social circle outside of their colleagues and own families. Those associated with SPC, however, are seen differently; they enjoy respect, recognition and even aid from the community for their contribution to the programme.

However, many DIs feel that the criteria for student selection into SPC is in some ways not fair. They would not go so far as to say it is biased, but the general feeling is students who are not very efficient or outgoing are excluded. By doing this, SPC is defeating the very purpose of its existence—improving leadership qualities and preparing children to be upstanding model citizens of the future.

Retired ASNO Babu says, 'Why should such an effective programme be limited to only the "cream"? Why shouldn't it be available to "slow kids?"'

Many serving cops independently raised this point during conversations for this book and made an alternative suggestion to select eleven children each from the top and the bottom half of the 'rank list' for the twenty-two male and twenty-two female cadets from each SPC school. It would be interesting to see how these suggestions are implemented in the years to come.

In addition, they also questioned the logic of excluding individuals who are not fully fit mentally and physically. The general outlook is that such a programme can make the most difference to those who may otherwise not be considered efficient, capable or brilliant. For example, in Periyar High, a few students with disabilities were selected as SPC cadets in the first year of the programme.

The special education resource teacher at the school recounted the experiences of those students. One student had mild mental retardation, another had a hearing impairment and the third student had a learning disability. The student with a learning disability was dull and had a speech impairment that led to her being labelled as intellectually challenged. IQ assessments, however, showed that her apparent dullness was because of her learning disability. All three students would participate in all the parades. The child with a hearing impairment was initially unable to perform the basic parade and asked to sit out by the DI involved. However, when the special education resource teacher at the school informed the DI that the child had a mild learning disability as well, the DI included her in the parade and gave her special coaching to get her up to speed with other cadets.

These parades taught all three children to do things in a time-bound manner—getting up in the morning, being punctual and so on. It also helped them to follow instructions and do activities in coordination with others. It brought rhythm to their life. The change it brought to the sense of self, the confidence and efficiency of the cadets, especially the one with a learning disability, was tremendous and she blossomed in the two years that she was part of SPC. This was quoted as a prime example of the difference SPC could make to someone who would otherwise be screened out of the programme. Similar sentiments were expressed by many who are still in the force and some who have superannuated.

There is another dialogue that might be of interest and use to SPC in the coming years—the question of better or equal representation of women in the mentoring arena. As of now, most DIs and senior board members are male, possibly due to the sheer prominence of men in the force. It could also be that the authority a man brings to the project is deemed superior to that brought in by a woman of the same age, rank and seniority. However, when the focus is on building a better democracy through improved leadership, the question of women representation poses a serious question. Women are an equal part of the citizenry and SPC, with its focus on empowering citizens of the future, has a definite need to allow and even encourage participation of women in the force. Since half of all cadets in the programme are women, it is important that the projected picture matches the actual status in the organisation.

5

Positivity and Possibilities
SPC's Impact on Society

The sense of unity that the SPC project brought into communities in Kerala is unparalleled in the history of Indian education. For instance, a SPC programme called 'Pos-Poss'—short for Positivity and Possibilities—was ideated and conceptualised during the pandemic in 2020 when in-person gatherings and interaction among cadets, CPOs and DIs were no longer possible. Rather than lamenting over the difficult times, Vijayan initiated a different way of maintaining and improving involvement of stakeholders in the training and development of the young cadets. Pos-Poss, an online talk show hosted by a non-profit Mission Better Tomorrow for SPC, had an average viewership of close to half a million.

Topics for discussion usually revolved around questions of leadership, leadership skills and problems young people should be solving today. Through these talks, SPC kids engaged with public and social issues. Chosen cadets were given the opportunity to interact with luminaries in different fields, which helped boost their confidence levels. This not only benefitted the cadets but the community at large since they got to listen to in-depth perspectives of experts that helped expand their worldview as well. The entire SPC community, including graduates, people associated with SPC in limited capacity and current cadets and their families came together, setting aside their perceived differences and tuning into these periodic conversations on positivity and possibility. These interactions also fundamentally altered the way police in Kerala saw themselves; rather than having the restricted vision of being enforcers of the law of the land, they now see themselves as active participants in social change.

SPC has become a framework with which schools are providing young people tremendous opportunities to do something meaningful and worthy in their life. Most cadets have either gone ahead and done something extraordinary or have shaped themselves into changemakers wherever they are. The alumni programme—originally named Pioneers and now called the SVC (Student Volunteer Corps)—has students working for causes because social commitment has become a large part of who they are. These volunteers go out of the way to make time and put in effort to work on SPC projects because they feel SPC played a great role in shaping them to be the better, socially productive youngsters they are today. They now look for ways to give back to the society and, in their own way, mentor younger cadets.

Today, teachers openly remark about the difference SPC has made in the academic performance of participating students. For instance, CPO Anver says that before SPC, his school could only hope for one or two students to get an A+ in all subjects in the board exams—a condition that changed dramatically since the advent of SPC in his school. According to him, ever since SPC was introduced, there has been a steady improvement in the discipline and academic performance of students, and not just among the SPC cadets.

Over the years, SPC has organically evolved a framework wherein children are being invited to be 'co-governors of the social'. One of the aims of this experiment in Kerala is to 'empower' women by ensuring their active participation in public places and political institutions through local self-governance. In this context, SPC has been able to bring about transformations in the student community, such as improved academic performance, tackling deviant behaviour and the empowerment of girl students who are trained in self-defense. Female cadets highlighted sexual exploitation of girls as the central theme of a musical skit performed during the second Annual Day functions of SPC conducted in Kochi on 25 August 2012. It outlined how girls who were once prey to sexual exploitation could now, because of their participation in SPC, actively fight off their exploiters and protect other girls (non-cadets) too.

An interesting dialogue in the community took place in connection with regard to the SPC uniform. While it may be argued that the SPC uniform is gender neutral, some may see it as masculine. Male and female cadets wear the exact same uniform: khaki pants with shirts tucked in, khaki-coloured socks and black shoes, black belt, lanyard with whistle, SPC lettering, name plate and a beret with the SPC insignia. There is also a PT uniform, comprising a white t-shirt with the SPC logo, black sweatpants, black socks and white canvas shoes. Cadets wear this during games, cross-country running and other physical activities. The khaki uniform had immense appeal for the cadets and it was, in fact, the reason that attracted many students to SPC.

Syam was a junior cadet who joined SPC but was limited to online activities due to the pandemic. He laments the fact that he has never been able to wear the uniform and parade in public. He waxed poetic about the SPC shoes that were given to him and his daily ritual of taking them out and polishing them before keeping them aside again and his longing for the opportunity to wear the SPC uniform and be recognised in it. Here, the role of the khaki in distinguishing SPC cadets from ordinary children is emphasised, while simultaneously stressing the contribution of the khaki in fashioning cadets who can discipline and govern the body politic. While the uniform definitely posed an allure for both male and female cadets, the opportunity to wear a masculine uniform, to simulate the police and the constitutive address of others recognising them as such had a unique significance for female cadets in a conservative society like Kerala. They were open and enthusiastic about the sense of authority the uniform provided them; perhaps the 'manliness' of the uniform had a role to play in this. Or, maybe the uniform simply allowed them to show how they truly felt about themselves free of the bonds societal norms placed on young girls. This is yet another example of the tangential way in which SPC provided possibilities to students they would not have been able to access otherwise.

The khaki uniform conferred prestige upon both male and female cadets; however, the ways in which the uniform mediated the female cadets' experiences with the world was different from that of the boys. It offered the girls visibility, power, authority and dignity. They were often mistaken for 'real police', and they delightedly recollected incidents of men in two-wheelers donning helmets as they approached, discarding their cigarettes out of respect for an 'officer' and not passing the kind of comments—often sexually explicit—usually flung at girls walking on the streets. Being able to traverse social spaces with assured dignity enabled them to feel they had a role in society. But in a society where girls in pants/jeans and shirts were still a rare sight, much less girls wearing well-fitted pants with tucked-in shirts, the uniform also became a source of anxiety.

References to the uniform were critical in elaborating the appeal of the cadets, with emphasis on the experiences of being a girl in Kerala. The uniform, a symbol of both restriction and liberation, impacts the girls' sociability (interactions and relationships with others) and mobility (ability to move and navigate through society). At the same time, it also shapes their sensibilities or perception about their role and position in society. The role of the uniform in the transformation of the child into a cadet, the discomfort that dressing in khaki aroused in particular girls and how those fears were marginalised in the name of discipline all made the uniform simultaneously liberating and constraining.

For these young girls, growing up in a patriarchal society means messages like 'boys will be boys', 'girls should be quiet and not make noise' and 'to make noise is to invite attention, and to invite attention is dangerous for a girl' are the norm. In this context, it is important to mention the confidence, relief and safety as well as pride that the SPC uniform provides. Many of the girls mention that areas and situations where they would otherwise face wolf whistles, groping or heckling are safe for them now simply because of the uniform, which begets them the respect they believe they deserve.

In her doctoral thesis, Dr Ann Mary Chacko quotes a focus group discussion with ex-female cadets belonging to tribal communities in Kabani High School. This is what Geetu had to say:

> When I return home from [the] parade in the evenings, it will be almost seven and then there will mostly be only men in the buses. Then the uniform is a source of courage. The driver and the ticket collector will say, 'police are coming, please move aside.' When we hear that we feel very courageous. We can get home in peace. In today's society, we can expect anything. Even in the school uniform we do not feel so courageous. But when we go in a police uniform, we feel as if this uniform is imbuing courage in us. Wherever it is, we have the [ability] to say 'don't touch'.
>
> In fact, when I return home after the parade in the evenings I always go back home in my [khaki] uniform, I never change into colour [regular dress], I feel very scared.

Sreeja, another SPC female cadet from the same school shared her story.

> There are both boy and girl cadets in SPC. But it is the girls that everyone notices. I have often wondered why? It is because boys usually get to wear it [the khaki]. When we say police, we immediately think of boys. We don't think of women. That's what is special. When we walk everyone looks at girls in amazement.

The female cadets are all aware of the fact that though everyone deserves to be treated with respect, under normal circumstances, it does not quite happen. However, the uniform affords them that respect and most of the female cadets who use public transport or walk home choose to wear their SPC uniform after a day of training since it ensures them safety from demeaning behaviour by men and boys. In that respect, the uniform acts as their saviour in a way that boys would not experience or understand.

Somehow, this uniform brought the girls a sense of freedom that allowed them to think and dream beyond what they thought was possible—to aspire for careers and public service instead of marriage and babies. This is precisely what allowed Amitha Fathima to dream big and entertain a vision of giving back to the nation. Amitha had just been transferred to St Anne's in Kottayam for Class XI when one of her classmates shocked her by saying that her name sounded like that of a terrorist. Instead of withdrawing into herself and wallowing in the pain the cutting comment caused, she decided that she would go out of her way to make that same student understand that she, Amitha, was larger than the stereotype. She chose to befriend the young girl who made that casual remark and show her how she was more than just a name—that she was a citizen and a responsible one, while also being just another regular girl of her age group.

When we look into the community at large, we see and hear stories of many parents who have more than one child in SPC; some have two kids in SPC at the same time while some others have one in SPC as another graduates and moves on to SVC. It speaks greatly of the project as a whole that parents who have had one child as part of the SPC would certainly want the next one also to be involved in the project. As Shakespeare wrote in *Twelfth Night*, 'Some are born great, some achieve greatness, and some have greatness thrust upon 'em.' In these pages, you'll meet a cadet from a GHSS Meppadi in Wayanad who came into the fold of SPC because she was inspired by her elder sibling.

Then there is Myzria, who survived a landslide and made her way back to the community after sprinting to the jungle when the disaster struck. That in itself would have been a great deed, but this young SPC went on to don the uniform she had kept at school and take care of those who were given shelter at that school following the disaster. She ensured a reading room was set up; she met and encouraged everyone to speak about their losses, fears, worries and hopes; she even made very detailed notes of these interactions showing amazing presence of mind and maturity. Such stories are not rare in the pages of SPC.

During the course of our fieldwork, we came across many parents who remained connected to SPC even after their children have graduated. Like the policemen who retired and still stayed in touch, these parents also retained their involvement in SPC activities so they were able to continue the work to which their children actively and sincerely contributed.

Also take the case of Adiya who decided to make over a hundred three-layered masks for the police constables on duty around her neighbourhood during the pandemic. Her grandmother chipped in and the duo decided to supply cool buttermilk to the cops on duty in the sweltering heat; they did that for two months with no expectations and without remuneration, earning the undying gratitude of the cops in her neighbourhood.

There are also some outstanding CPOs who come up with fantastic ways of giving back to the community. Take the example of Mini, a CPO who donated a kidney, her hair and a part of her liver. Another CPO, Anver, has made it his life's work to ensure the community learns and thrives through farming and fishing.

With all the positive stories being shared, it may seem that every single student who participated in the SPC programme has done great in life, but in all honesty, there have been some lost sheep along the way. The phenomenal wins enjoyed by SPC have positioned such losses and failures in sharp contrast, hitting the leadership really hard. The tragedy of losing a cadet to drug abuse—even though the team struggled as one to free them—has left deep scars in the hearts and minds of all those who associated with them.

Such instances bring into focus the vagaries of the community we still live in. In many cases, when a CPO identifies 'strangeness' in a cadet's behaviour and tries to bring that to the notice of their parents, they face resistance from the parents. The same parents, in some cases, return with tears in their eyes to apologise and request help from the CPO, but on most occasions, it becomes a case of too little, too late. It is noteworthy that cases of drug abuse fail to be noticed or reported by neighbours in cities more than in rural areas—the sense of community seems to be one of the deciding factors in catching them early in the habit.

Unfortunately, such events do occur and they weigh on the hearts of the CPOs and DIs, but every such experience spurs them on to do more. CPOs, through their interactions with the police force, have learnt more ways of dealing with troubled teens than a teachers' way of reporting them to higher authorities or parents. Their link with the police force allows them to bring in a greater element of credibility when they talk to youngsters about possible entanglements and repercussions in matters other than studies.

The community that comprises parents, teachers and students working together for the greater good of all is the same community that will produce brilliant leaders and great citizens of tomorrow. SPC is doing its part in shaping such a community, and it is up to decision-makers in organisation to look into these pages and decide how to plug the holes that have come to light at this point. Just like how some of the simple projects within SPC have stretched their boundaries and grown to much larger proportions, it is up to the leadership to support, mentor and allow SPC to continue to grow beyond its current limitations.

The stories that follow are just a few of the thousands that SPC habours; this book is only a fleeting glimpse of the wonder that SPC is. We bring these to you with the fervent hope that these stories inspire you to be better than we are and to allow our light to shine as long and as brightly as it can.

Section II
Success Stories of SPC

6

Success Story 1
Conserving the Future

The children were assembled at GHHS Pattikad in Thrissur district to observe World Environment Day on 5 June.

This day is observed in schools across India to generate awareness about the role that human beings must play in the protection and preservation of their immediate natural environment, especially in the context of rapid urbanisation and spread of industries and businesses that exploit natural resources for sustenance. Events such as these help children gain awareness of the importance of sustainable development, which proposes that dwindling natural resources should be used optimally to ensure their preservation for future generations. It is a step towards achieving the SDGs implemented by the United Nations Development Programme. These events have helped the behavioural change of students by fostering environmental ethics and values.

The event was underway. The children had gathered to plant some saplings but were taken aback when they dug up the ground. One of the cadets, Teeshma Abraham, recalls the day, 'We dug a pit to plant one sapling and were shocked to find it full of plastic waste.'

This was what prompted the beginning of a change. The children were so disappointed by how much damage was being done to their natural environment that they thought of doing something about it. After discussing it among themselves, they went to the headmistress and got permission to start collecting plastic waste from the school premises and from their homes as an intervention. When they began, they were able to collect 120 kilograms of plastic waste in a day and send away three truckloads for recycling.

This led to the birth of the Mukti programme aimed at waste management by cadets from GHHS Pattikad. This school is situated close to the Peechi Dam, which provides drinking water to Thrissur, the fourth-largest city and third-largest urban agglomeration in Kerala with a population of more than 1,80,000. Peechi Dam, which is twenty-two kilometres from Thrissur's centre, is a famous tourist attraction. The dam is of historical importance for the people of this city. It was inaugurated in 1957 after ten years of construction initiated by the then Prime Minister of the state, Kochi E. Ikkanda Warrier. The dam is the largest source of irrigation as well as drinking water for the people in this region. Owing to the huge influx of tourists, there are many food stalls around the dam that causes accumulation of food and plastic waste in the area.

People in the villages and areas neighbouring the Peechi Dam had grown accustomed to piles of garbage, especially plastic, that was being dumped there every day. It was the obvious result of Peechi Dam being a popular tourist site. But for Nandini, a CPO at GHHS Pattikad, this was unacceptable. She quickly realised that normalising garbage dumps in the area would only increase the negative impact on the environment.

Across Kerala, waste management has been a serious issue, and governments over the years have made rigorous efforts to turn the situation around by initiating various waste management projects. But the Mukti programme stands out as it was spearheaded and sustained by students. It sprouted out of the realisation that the natural resources need to be preserved for the future and the preparation for the same needs to be started today.

Nandini, who was guiding her peers through their journey in the Mukti programme, knew that there would be challenges and opposition. Even though agriculture is the main source of income for people in and around the Peechi Dam area, the use of plastic was just as high as anywhere else in the state and its disposal unplanned and thus highly reckless. Heaps of plastic waste could be seen dumped everywhere and this situation was exacerbated by the waste left behind by tourists who came to visit the dam. This needed positive action by the locals, and Nandini played a pivotal role in mobilising students in attempting to resolve this. The SPC at her school provided her with the right platform to spearhead the Mukti initiative. She mobilised the cadets and made a trial attempt. The cadets moved around the village and collected abandoned plastic.

The magnitude of the issue became visible when, in just two days of random waste collection, more than 300 kilograms of waste was collected. Nandini realised that the management of this effort was way beyond the capacity of the school or the cadets.

Soon, Kudumbasree members and accredited social health activists (ASHAs)—community health workers designated by the union government's Ministry of Health and Family Welfare (MoHFW) as part of the National Rural Health Mission (NRHM)—were brought into the picture. A list of 150 persons was made to collect plastic waste. But these collectors or Mukti volunteers could not sort the plastic. Consequently, Mukti entered into a contract with two dealers to do this job.

Before the academic session ended that year, cadets from GHHS Pattikad collected thirty tonnes of plastic waste from the village and disposed of it safely. This led to grama sabhas coming forward to open secondary collection centres across the panchayat on weekends.

Soon, the residents of Pattikad also started supporting the venture. The support began as a trickle, as it is always with any social movement, but gathered momentum. Cadets met and talked about the project at thirty-two gram sabhas. Madrasas and churches in the area extended full support. Mukti got sponsors for the work. People came forward with food for the children who were collecting the waste or provided garbage bags. The public was made aware of the sorting process. The plastic waste divided into seven categories: bottles, aluminium foil, milk packets, medicine packaging and three sets of plastic bags, depending on their micron values.

Volunteers from all over Pattikad came to the school to hand over the plastic they had collected. The collection drive would take place between 7.30 a.m. and 9 a.m. By evening, carts filled with sacks of plastic waste would leave the school premises.

Then, something remarkable happened. A team from Universal Records Forum (URF), a society that documents and supports unique efforts for their endurance and achievement, was visiting the neighbourhood. URF was documenting Marottichal village in the neighbouring Puthur panchayat which staked the claim of being 'the first fully chess-literate village in the world'. Umesh A., the then Circle Inspector (CI) of Ollur, was interacting with the URF team when he informed them about Pattikad and its enterprising kids. Umesh was the Police Student Liaison Officer (PSLO) for the school.

'It helped in a way that [the] children started to document the extraordinary work they [had] been doing in a proper and systematic way for the URF authorities to verify. [URF] evaluated the activities for six months and awarded the certificate in 2016,' says Umesh.

He remembers incentivising this for the children. Bicycles, umbrellas and bags were distributed among students who collected the maximum volume of clean and recyclable plastic. Teeshna was the first to win a bicycle for bringing in 500 kilograms of plastic. 'There was resistance and criticism in the beginning when people saw kids picking up waste,' he says.

However, the real success of Mukti was not in organising a system to collect the plastic waste from different points of the panchayat, but in making the residents aware of the ill-effects of indiscriminate use of plastic and the irresponsible dumping of it. Once the SPC and Mukti volunteers started moving around the panchayat, meeting social leaders and residents to talk about the garbage menace that loomed large over their lives, people started to think.

Once the thought is triggered, action follows. Soon, the volume of plastic coming to the school came down drastically. Earlier, four to five loads of garbage used to be removed at the end of every day's collection. Soon, it came down to just one carrier vehicle leaving the school.

The change was so obvious that the other schools in the neighbourhood also volunteered to join the movement. By then, the total collection of plastic garbage in one academic year dipped from thirty to eighteen tonnes.

The SPC has invoked the innate potential of taking a lead in social movements. Once the system for proper management of plastic waste in and around Peechi Dam was in place, the focus shifted to vegetable farming on school premises. Results started showing when organic farming brought in a profit of ₹32,000 to the school.

It was just an indication of the times to come. The profit from the vegetable farming in the school was handed over to the Adivasi (Tribal) Settlement Centre at Attappady as a support fund for better nutrition to the anaemic children in the community. The virtue of a movement that started off as an attempt to resolve a social issue began influencing people in many unexpected ways.

Teachers in the school were given training in making paper pens and cloth bags. Children were taught to be gentle with nature and more responsive to social issues. Umesh concludes by saying,

More than just removing the plastic, what the kids did was amazing. Peechi is home to many endangered plant species, which are endemic to that region. A couple more years of pollution at that scale would have wiped off many species forever. Without actually knowing it, the children were conserving the precious and indigenous plant variety of the region.

Children of this school took the lead and claimed the ownership of the programme, but soon the entire locality joined in. The Mukti programme remains a successful one that invoked people's sense of responsibility towards their environment, leading to behavioural change.

7

Success Story 2

The Red Night in Forest

Deep inside the forests, the nights are long and cold. The darkness is haunting, the silence is eerie. The dead of the night hides many mysteries. For those of us who do not know what lies inside the forest, the journey inside can be unnerving. But for Surya, the forest was her home. She had been brought up here; she knew all its nooks and crannies and was not afraid of it.

In India, there are about 68 million people belonging to 227 ethnic groups, comprising 573 tribal communities that live primarily in forested regions. In fact, India is home to some of the most primitive and vulnerable tribes in the world. A characteristic of tribal communities living in India is that they remain cut off from mainstream culture and can exhibit reluctance in terms of adopting modern socio-economic and educational approaches. These communities still adhere to ancient and intrinsic regulations and play a very important role in the preservation of the biodiversity since they worship the forests that they dwell in.

Surya belongs to the matrilineal Kurichiya tribe, one among the twenty-odd Scheduled Tribes living inside forests of Kerala.

The Kurichyars are known to be reclusive and hesitant in their interactions with outsiders.

Despite the fact that Surya belonged to this tribe, she did interact with the outside world and recognised how different it was from her community. Since 2013, she had been attending the GHHS at Thalappuzha, a small village in Wayanad. The school was around six kilometres from Makkimala, where her house was among four others tucked inside a dense forest.

One night, the usual calm was disrupted when five strangers came knocking at their door. Over the years, such visits to their settlements had become a routine and people would usually open their doors to welcome such uninvited guests, even if reluctantly. These guests would come with leaflets and talk about the injustices that they had been facing as tribals. They would ask for food, which was a scarce commodity for these people. And then, following such visits the police would invariably visit the homes where these visitors had stayed to inquire about what had happened.

In India, these 'visitors' are known as Maoists. They are essentially political activists operating out of forests who believe in the form of communism developed by Mao Tse Tung. The philosophy of Maoists is that of critiquing social inequalities promoted through state policies. They believe in an armed struggle to ensure that their rights are protected. In doing so, they have, over the years, been in confrontation with the state forces, leading to much collateral damage. As a result, people living in Maoist areas are afraid of such visits to their homes.

Surya was scared of both Maoists and the police. But this feeling for her changed when she joined SPC in 2013. She had learnt in school that as the citizen of a state, she was entitled to certain rights and that the state was obligated to provide them for her protection. This made her feel more secure. As a cadet, the more she interacted with police officers associated with the SPC project, the more her fears dissipated.

She realised that if the police were there to protect her and her family, they would not let her become a victim of collateral damage in any confrontation between them and the Maoists. So, that night, when the five Maoists came to her home, Surya was able to keep her calm.

Among the five guests, Surya was able to recognise Roopesh and Sundari. This was because her father, who worked as a watcher with the Department of Forests, used to bring home notices issued by the government, which contained photos of known Maoists.

Roopesh was a law graduate with a diploma in information technology. He and his wife Shyna, an employee of the High Court of Kerala, had been accused of Maoist activities in Tamil Nadu, Kerala and Karnataka.

'They told us that they were not there to hurt us. They just wanted to spread awareness about some issues concerning them. They gave us pamphlets and spent some time before leaving,' said Surya about the visit.

The Maoists looked tired and drained after what might have been many days of walking in the wilderness. Surya's mother gave them hot tea to drink, which they were grateful for.

Surya, who was very confident at that time owing to her involvement with the SPC, was interested in the arms these guests were carrying and asked if she could have a look at the gun. Not used to such candid interactions, the guests exchanged surprised smiles among themselves. Then, one of them, a woman with bright eyes, handed over the gun to Surya. As she took the gun from her hand, Surya remembered that she had seen the woman before.

The woman removed the cartridge before giving the gun to Surya. But the gun was too heavy for Surya to lift. She rested the gun on her right shoulder, held it with her left hand at the fore-end. She closed one eye and took aim. When she did that with precision, the guest were shocked.

Surya took the gun off her shoulder and weighed it once more before returning it. The woman who gave her the gun was not smiling any more. Instead, she looked firmly into Surya's eyes.

'Are you not Sundari?' Surya asked.

There was no answer but when Surya looked around, there was a strange silence. The visitors were no longer comfortable.

'How do you know me?' she asked Surya.

'I have seen your photograph,' said Surya.

Sundari was a prominent member of the Communist Party of India (Maoist) (CPI-M) South Zonal Committee. She, along with six others like Vikram Gowda and Soman, top leaders of the committee, entered the forests of Nilambur following the death of their leaders, Kuppu Devaraj and Ajitha, in a police encounter in 2016.

Kuppu Devaraj, a central committee member of the CPI(M), had been in charge of the tri-junction area of Karnataka, Kerala and Tamil Nadu for over a decade. He had been a native of Krishnagiri in Tamil Nadu and was heading the operations south of Mangaluru when he was killed in a police encounter. Police sources tracked his presence in Tamil Nadu, around Ooty and in forests of Kerala. His death, along with that of Ajitha, stirred up ruckus and most people refrained from any unnecessary interaction with them.

But this time, Surya had interacted in a way that the visitors were not familiar with. They stood up as soon as they finished drinking the tea. From their shoulder bags, they fished out some leaflets on forest fires and how to minimise their risk. Unlike other times, they did not say a word about the insurgency, or revolution as they called it, or ask the villagers about police presence or movement in the area.

Just as they were leaving, Sundari turned back and gave Surya a quick glance. Surya could not understand it. Later, the policemen told Surya and the other cadets that the Maoists had visited some other villages and told the locals that they would avenge the deaths of Kuppu Devaraj and Ajitha. In this case, however, the group left after collecting rice and other essential material. Surya was not surprised seeing them leave in a hurry. It was because she had identified Sundari. But she was not afraid anymore. She knew she could stand up and ask questions if they came back.

Surya was the first cadet from her hamlet to join the force at GHSS Thalappuzha. The SPC programme had started at the school in 2010 and Surya joined as Junior SPC in 2014. Her confidence and transformation as a leader inspired many other students. In 2020, there were six cadets from Makkimala, which is a huge achievement.

The next day in school, Surya reported the matter to DI Mathew N.J. and the assistant sub-inspector of the Thalappuzha station. Mathew asked her to keep quiet about the incident; he reported it to the department. This led to the first case to be registered against Roopesh under the Unlawful Atrocities Prevention Act (UAPA) in Thalappuzha. Roopesh and Shyna were arrested in 2015 and are currently facing trial.

Mathew remembers Surya as a very brave girl.

Many years later, as she recollected that night, Surya said that she had been under the impression that Maoists were terrifying, but that night, she understood that they were just regular people. The only difference was that they were wasting their time resorting to armed violence from within the forest rather than engaging with the government using resources available with the system.

Even as a new mother to a newborn, Surya fondly keeps her old SPC uniform. She dreams of getting back to an SPC-type of leadership role in the near future after fulfilling her homemaker roles in her husband's household.

She feels that the urge to stand up against injustice and stop people from doing the wrong thing is very much in her. The uniform that gave her the courage to talk back to Maoists will guide her through the rest of her life. Once a SPC, always an SPC.

8

Success Story 3
That Long Beep in the Dark

The hike along the stone-paved track, long after the macadamised road ended, wound through the tribal hamlet at Thadikund in Palakkad. Thatched huts punctuated the solid, concrete single-room houses with dish antennae. A dog growled from the verandah, while a lazy buffalo watched. At the farthest end of the colony was a football ground, around which was a plastic net tied to the poles to stop the ball from going over to the steep ridge beyond.

T. Satyan, the principal-in-charge of the GVHSS, stood at the edge of the ground and pointed downwards to the valley. There, deep down through the wilderness, Bhavani River could be seen flowing. There was a bamboo footbridge that looked quite tiny from this height. He said, 'The vehicles could go only up to that area, right near the footbridge. The kids from the hamlet led the election literacy team, carrying the voting machines, directing them to the hamlets and helped demonstrate how the machines worked.'

Satyan also was the master trainer of the Electoral Literacy Club. The forests around the Bhavani and Siruvani Rivers are home to three main tribal communities: Irulas, Kurumba and Muthuka. Thadikund is one of the nineteen settlement areas for Kurumba, the most primitive tribe and the earliest inhabitants of the Attappady area in Palakkad. Attappady is home to a protected forest and hosts 192 tribal hamlets. However, migration practices among tribals in Attappady have caused the population to shrink by nearly 90 per cent since 1951.

This community is generally known to not engage in political processes and the members are reluctant to cast their votes during elections. Their general apathy towards electoral politics was further compounded with the introduction of electronic voting machines, which were completely new to them, having lived in their own world away from modernity and with almost no exposure to new technologies. There was also the fear of Maoist presence in the forest which made the tribal communities more reclusive.

The electoral officers in Palakkad consequently believed that with the introduction of electronic voting machines and voter-verified paper audit trail (VVPAT), the tribal communities would be further alienated from the process.

But Satyan and his students were not going to let this happen. During the 2019 general elections, they took models of the electronic voting machine and VVPAT to the tribal colonies deep inside the forest and demonstrated how to use them. In the first batch, twenty-six students were trained on how to use the new system. These children then trained others before forming groups with grown-ups to venture deep into the tribal hamlets.

Their task was two-fold.

First, to ease the tribal communities out of their inherent fear of the outside world. Here, it is important to understand that among Adivasi communities in Kerala, there is a general reluctance to emerge from their secure social world. Even in schools, tribal children mostly prefer to mingle with other tribal children rather than with students from other communities. As such, most of the kids facilitating the sessions on election processes were from these tribal communities and this helped greatly. They were able to speak in the indigenous language that helped ease the locals.

The second task was to make the tribal communities aware of their democratic rights. Leaflets on how to use the electronic voting machine were distributed, along with the actual demonstration of it. Satyan recollects an incident that highlights the importance of communicating with the tribals in their indigenous language. The team was going into the forest when they spotted a group of tribal women. They stopped and started to explain why they were there. The response was a barrage of complaints about how the tribe lacked vital facilities despite offers made by the elected governments. 'Why should we vote?' was the common refrain.

The officers were at a loss of words. But Rajeswary M., a Class X cadet who belonged to the Irula tribe, stepped in and without losing a moment, began explaining the entire electoral process in their language. She was able to win the confidence of the women and convince them.

Suman Sachdeva, an Echidna research fellow at the Brookings Institute, notes that language remains a significant barrier for children from Adivasi communities trying to access education as a pathway to empowerment.

The pedagogical barriers refer primarily to the teaching and learning transactions that happen in schools with large populations of Adivasi children. These schools have few teachers from the tribal communities who can understand the language of children in a classroom. They are thus taught mostly by non-tribal teachers, who often have low expectations of their ability to learn. This reinforces feelings of unworthiness, which can be especially harmful for girls from excluded communities who already face the social barrier.[1]

Recalling this encounter with tribal women, Rajeswari said, 'I did not know what I was thinking at that point. We were not prepared for such an encounter. But I felt that I should step in and take control of the situation as any attempt to explain in a language that is not their own would have aggravated the situation.' Rajeswari pulled out the dummy machine and demonstrated how it worked. Right there, in the middle of the jeep track to the tribal hamlet.

The result of this initiative by SPC from GVHSS Agali can be seen in voting outcome. There was a 14 per cent increase in votes polled.[2] For example, the tribal hamlet at Murukula,

---

[1] https://www.brookings.edu/blog/education-plus-development/2015/09/29/will-we-ever-be-able-to-read-barriers-for-tribal-girls-in-india/]

[2] https://www.thehindu.com/news/national/kerala/attappady-spc-on-cloud-nine/article26936150.ece

which is twelve kilometres from the nearest polling booth and tucked deep in the forest, recorded 98 per cent polling from tribal hamlets, with only two persons failing to make it to the polling booth as they were hospitalised at the time.

The Chindakki polling station, which covers 10 tribal colonies, registered a first-time ever figure of 73.08 per cent polling. 'This was totally unprecedented, as Chindakki [has] never [recorded] anything over 60 per cent. The children did a remarkable job this year,' said a proud Satyan.

Election officials were only happy to support this energy-packed group. The region was selected after intense discussion between the assistant superintendent, the district collector and Navaneeth Sharma, IPS and the entire area was subjected to detailed combing to eliminate any security threat to the children, and they were allowed to proceed only after ensuring their full security. It was Sharma who entrusted four teams of Kerala Thunderbolts to move along with the children. Kerala Thunderbolts is an elite commando force of the Kerala Police set up in accordance with the union government's directions after the 26/11 Mumbai terror attacks in 2008. The commando force's mandate is to counter possible terror strikes and carry out counterinsurgency operations in Kerala.

'We were provided with adequate protection, which included four Thunderbolt teams. The children were really persuasive or else we could not have made this. All the twenty voters in twenty hamlets at Mutukula were adamant on not voting. Eventually, they did,' said G. Shaju, former president of the PTA at the school.

The SPC made a drastic contribution to raising awareness on the use of electronic voting machines among tribal communities. Members of the tribes were able to freely communicate with these children and this helped with a surprisingly high voter turn-out. The students' spirits were high and they really pushed themselves to make this initiative a success. Challenges were met head on and no obstacle was big enough to make them stop.

Take the examples of Ajith Francis's team and four other boys who went to the Chundikulam tribal colony where they met 104-year-old Nanchiyamma. She told them that she would not come to vote but was eventually convinced. But on the polling day, they could not find her at the booth. So, they went back to her hamlet and brought her along. Halfway, she realised that she had forgotten to take along her Aadhaar card. So, the boys climbed back to her house on a hillock, looked all over the place and brought the card to her booth for voting. She was escorted back to her home in the official jeep after the voting.

Later, Nanchiyamma, proud of her small feat, would re-enact how she voted using the electronic voting machine. Remembering the long beep from the machine that confirmed her vote would lead her to squeal in childlike laughter. She proudly claims to have cast her vote in all elections ever since.

Nothing like this had ever happened before. The system took note of the magnitude of change these kids had brought about in a place as remote as the tribal hamlets of Attappady. The governor of Kerala held a special session on National Voters' Day (celebrated on 25 January) at the historic VJT Hall, Trivandrum in 2020 to honour those who worked on this huge changemaking initiative. Along with Loknath Behra, the state police chief and P. Vijayan, IG and state nodal officer of SPC, fifty-two proud children from GVHSS, Agali, and their four teachers, stood in the spotlight. The mementoes and certificates in their hands were no match for the gleam of pride on their faces. Satyan submitted a detailed report on the incident earlier in New Delhi when he represented Palakkad at the Electoral Literacy Club meeting, and the Election Commission of India acknowledged that it was a great work that the teachers and kids had done.

> The Electoral Literacy Club (ELC) programme was launched by the President of India on National Voters Day of 2018. They are informal learning groups which being set up across the country as direct interventions of Election Commission of India for promoting electoral literacy among Indian citizens of all ages by engaging them in interesting and experiential hands-on learning activities in their local languages in a strictly apolitical, non-partisan and neutral manner.[3]

There was a big learning lesson for the state in the task accomplished by the student cadets. This was noted in *My Vote Matters*, the quarterly magazine of the Election Commission of India. The August 2021 edition carried the success story of Rajeshwari and her friends in detail.

> The success of the Attappady model emanated from its participatory nature. It teaches policy makers that any initiative seeking the participation of people should be sensitive to their cultural, political, social and economic

---

[3] https://ecisveep.nic.in/articles.html/new-initiative/electoral-literacy-clubs-r20/

needs. In order to consistently achieve higher voter turnout, it is important to respond effectively to the social and developmental needs of tribes in Attappady.

This exercise was an eye-opener for many students too. They got insight into why tribal folks had no trust in the system. 'How could they [earlier] when they [had] to tie up dead bodies of their dear ones to bamboo stretchers and carry [them] all the way to the hospital for post-mortem?' asked Divya, a cadet involved in the programme.

With a twinkle in her eye, Rajeswari says,

These people came out of their world to vote because they trusted our words. They believed in us, when we spoke in their languages and explained that vote was the key to their being part of the system. Now, it is time for them to ask questions on what happens after voting. We will go back to them, get their complaints and demands noted and forward it to the authorities. That was a promise we made to them and we will fulfil it.

With help from teachers like Satyan and Joseph Antony, the cadets from GVHSS, Agali, are now planning to compile a long list of needs that the tribal community demands of the democratic system since they have taken a deliberate decision to come forward to join the system. Proper roads and better connectivity top the list, say the children. 'We have relatives in these colonies, and so, we keep visiting them,' said Asaranya, a cadet.

The kids have won the confidence of the community like never before. Radha, a student police cadet, wants to become an airhostess, an ambition beyond the imagination of the community. But these children are now taking back nuggets of the new world they experienced back to their hamlets, opening up amazing vistas of exchange. The cadets want the adults to respond and take this engagement to the next level. Winning the confidence was just the first step, maintaining it is going to be the real deal.

9

Success Story 4
When Trees Rushed Down the Hill

Meppadi is a slice of heaven. There is always a chill in the air, winning it the name 'Poor Man's Ooty'. Nestled between two hills, Meppadi chugs along at a languid pace by the state highway that connects Kozhikode to Ooty. Most of the settlers here are migrant workers employed at the tea estates.

But Meppadi's idyllic life would change during the second massive flood that shook Kerala. Wayanad and Meppadi were largely safe during the historic flood of 2018, but alerts were issued again when the rains returned in 2019. There was always a threat of landslides. But no one expected it to be this massive.

Before anyone realised, five lakh cubic tonnes of earth came down from the top of the hills, washing away sixty houses and killing seventeen persons. This incident took place on 7

August 2019. It had been pouring heavily for three days and 127 centimetres of rainfall was recorded in the region.

'We were standing in front of our house when we heard that huge cracking sound uphill. We looked up and saw the entire forest being washed down. It was like the trees were coming down the hill together. We only had time to scamper to safety,' said Saleema, one of the residents of Puthumala, which was the worst hit in the landslide. Within six minutes, Saleema and others lost everything they had built in their lives. An entire village was washed down in the landslide. Out of eighty houses, only ten survived. The entire landscape of Meppadi village was altered.

Saleema and family had moved to their relative's place on hearing the alert. For more than an hour, her daughter Myzria was missing. There was no way she could be searched for in the deluge and utter chaos around. But just then, the girl came running out of the forest, drenched to the bone.

This is Myzria's story of bravery and compassion, a model student cadet who stands out owing to her spirit to serve people.

Myzria remembers running without looking back. But all she had in mind was wanting to return to her parents. She pondered for a while about the possibility of being trapped in the forest and not being able to find the way back. But she survived that phase without panicking, thanks to her training as a student police cadet. After nearly an hour, she climbed through a path filled with thorny undergrowth. Soon, she reached a *paadi* or a settlement where she spotted familiar faces and then made her way back to her family.

The survivors in the neighbourhood were shifted to the nearby Mundukai Forest Office, along with Myzria and her family. There were around forty people, who had lost their homes, huddled inside the office for the night. The next day, they moved in with other survivors to the Meppadi GHSS. Myzria was a student police cadet in this school.

Her home was completely washed away and she had to stay with her family in one of her school's classrooms. But the cadet in Myzria could not rest and she immediately resorted to helping out others.

> There was a man who had lost his wife in the landslide, and he would keep crying inconsolably and never asked for anything. I used to sit with him to try and console him to bring him back to a normal state of mind.

Myzria had also lost everything, except an SPC uniform that she kept in school. She put that on and started working with the relief workers straight away.

Shafina, the elder sister of Myzria, was a student police cadet too. Myzria recalls being fascinated watching her sister in uniform. That had been her motivation to join when she entered Class VIII for the 2017-18 academic year. Initially, it had been hard to do parades on dusty grounds after school hours. But that was just in the beginning; later, she enjoyed being a part of the force.

Sabu M.P., president of PTA, remembers Myzria moving from one room to another, helping the survivors, asking what they needed and ensuring their demands were met. 'She was smiling all the while. She had such a reassuring impact on the relief camp.'

Myzria documented the human tragedies as a result of this natural disaster to the minutest detail. She gathered information from survivors and made it a point to write them down. Her notes show how four families were removed from the debris of their houses using ropes. They were first shifted to the house of a man named Usman and then to Puthumala Lower Primary School. 'Two persons from this camp returned to their homes to bring something. Their bodies are yet to be recovered,' she wrote.

Her notebook is filled with life stories like these. Take the story of Shoukath, who operated the canteen for tea estate workers at Palakkad. He and his wife Muneera were in the canteen when the landslide happened.

> Just before the landslide came, their son Chinnu (3 years) asked his mother to lie down with him for a while. But Muneera could not oblige because of the rush at the canteen. Chinnu was born after twelve years of marriage. He was washed away. Someone rescued Shoukath and Muneera from the deluge, leaving them to tell the tale.'

The school was now home to 650 people who had lost their homes in the calamity. The crisis was huge. There were only seven toilets available for this big a crowd. Myzria knew the magnitude of the tragedy, and she knew the people staying at her school. She kept her eyes and heart open to take in their stories and console the victims, all the while forgetting the troubles of her own family.

But the tragedy was too much for the school to handle it all by itself. Those like Ibrahim M.P., the staff secretary, were clueless about what to do. Ibrahim sent across a voice note to his contacts, giving an overview of the situation at the school and seeking support. This message went viral, and support started pouring in from all over the world. Soon, the school had a surplus of relief material, which was then diverted to other camps.

Abdul Saleem, sub-inspector of Meppadi Police Station, was the DI at GHSS Meppadi. He recollects:

Those in the relief camp were totally cut off from the outside world. I then thought that bringing them news from outside would relieve their tension a bit. When I discussed this with the school officials, the response was dull. Naturally, they were more concerned about immediate requirements like food and hygiene. All they could give me was one room where things were dumped. The SPCs of the school needed just about one-and-a-half hours to clean it up and set up the reading room, with all leading dailies donating newspapers and magazines for free. We ended up having more reading material than actually required, which we shared with other camps in the neighbourhood.

SPC was started in the school in 2012. Since then, it has taken the lead in instilling courage and leadership among its students. The cadets are eager to fight back the drug menace or streamline traffic in the school area. They never shy away from a task assigned to them.

In 2019, the World Health Organization did a survey on the high rates of non-communicable diseases in the region. Initially, the Department of Health tried to gather the data through ASHAs, the community health workers designated by the union government's MoHFW as part of the NRHM. But the formats were in English and the ASHA workers could not do the job. Mary Mathew, the headmistress of the school, recollects how 'our junior cadets were briefed about the data to be collected and the ways to do that. They completed the survey in just one day!'

But the floods of 2019 brought the best out of the cadets. Cadets were assigned to each classroom where survivors were put up. They were asked to be on the look-out for any disease outbreak and to ensure that the residents of the relief camp were provided with adequate food and clothing. They even ran to the reading room in an orderly manner. They were everywhere.

CPO, Dinesh T., says,

Finally, when the camp was disbanded, we realised that fifteen uniforms allotted to the SPCs were damaged because of over-exposure to bleaching powder, a major disinfectant used in the relief camps. Funds allotted for the uniform of SPCs remain limited, so children are still using those uniforms now. But they carry these stains as badges of honour.

The news about the work done by SPC at the relief camp spread and for those who came to help and support them, Myzria became an icon of resilience and courage in the times of tragedy.

The SPC unit of GHHS Vanmugham, Koyilandy, was immensely impressed by the work done by one of their counterparts and the graceful manner in which she stepped over her personal tragedy and espoused the true SPC spirit by surrendering herself to relief work. On returning to their base, they discussed Myzria's story and decided to start a collection to help her build a new home. The first instalment of the collection was handed over in March 2020.

Saleema recollects that after joining SPC in 2017–19, the change was obvious in her daughter. She became bold and was ever ready to step out to help others. Maybe it was that confidence that helped her find the way back after being lost in the forest in heavy rain and traumatised by the sight of the landslide washing away her home, after nearly an hour. That training also helped her put on her uniform with a smile and get to relief work without ruminating over what was lost.

It has definitely given her the vision to stay focused. 'I want to become an IPS officer so that I can be of help to those in need,' Myzria says.

10

Success Story 5
Fruits of Labour

Every time a situation looks bleak, know that there is a ray of light—somewhere. All it takes to find it is to depart from convention and uncover new ways of approaching a problem. That is what this story is about. This is the story of Anver, who sparked sustainable social change.

Anver had returned home after four years of teaching at Radhwa International School at Yanbu, a port city in Saudi Arabia. His new job as a teacher at GVHSS Vithura was not not particularly exciting but he was happy to be back home and grateful for it.

When he started his job at the school, he observed that the situation in the school was grim and needed a special intervention to bring about a change. Anver had studied in a school that was only thirteen kilometres away, so he could relate to the circumstances there. The children in the school were warm-hearted but there were serious issues of discipline and many young boys were delinquents involved in drug abuse. There were limited punitive and corrective measures against this at school and things were spinning out of control. Along with drug abuse, there were also other concerns like molestation and sexual harassment by the auto-rickshaw drivers and others in the locality. There were regular complaints from the female students at the school.

'There was no NSS or NCC at the school. So, when the local police superintendent gave us a demonstration on SPC, we found it really motivating,' Anver said.

Officers from the Vithura police station were given the duty to train the cadets. The project was as new to the police officers as it was for the school. At times, the officers could not find time to follow up on the training schedule diligently. But the school was lucky to get Baiju, the station writer, who volunteered to step in as the DI. Since he would spend most of his time inside the police station—his colleagues would be out on the field for patrolling and surveillance—he became interested in the role of the DI.

One of the first things that he and Anver did was to convene a meeting of auto-rickshaw drivers and shop owners around the school to report cases of molestation as well as drug abuse. Children were also made aware about the harms of using drugs. 'We interacted with them and once they realised the intentions of SPC, they became willing partners in the fight against narcotics and sexual abuse of children and would pass on information about anyone misbehaving with children,' said Anver.

That marked the first turn in the fortunes of the school. Next was when another officer from Vithura police station became the DI. Nizarudeen came from an agrarian family, and they had nearly an acre of paddy fields. 'During one of the interactions, I asked the cadets whether they knew about haystacks. They did not. That moment made me think. I wanted the kids to learn about our agriculture first-hand.' Nizarudeen's uncle allotted half an acre of his land to the SPC for teaching cadets about land use and agriculture.

Kids were taken to the field, which was just about seven kilometres away from the school, and provided with food and refreshments by the police officer. There, they were given basic lessons in planting the saplings, taking care of the nascent plants, nourishing them and finally harvesting. 'The harvest was inaugurated by the state minister for agriculture, as this was the first instance of SPCs venturing into agriculture. They harvested forty para of paddy from their field,' said a proud Nizaruddeen.

Anjali R.J. was one of the first SPCs to participate in this programme. She recollects fondly:

> It was for the first time that I was seeing a plough and bullock used in the paddy fields, not to mention having first-hand experience of using them. It was an experience that cannot be put in words, when we stood in the mud and planted the sapling against a thread drawn to keep the line straight.

Charged up by the success and the exhilarating experience, the cadets went further. Manoharan Nair, a local aqua farmer, became their guide. That he was an alumnus of the school helped more. In 2014, Nair and the student cadets got together and designed the Oru Nellu, Oru Meen (One Paddy, One Fish) project. The same half-acre land is being used alternately for growing paddy and aquaculture. The first harvest was in 2015 and it was unexpectedly successful. In fact, in 2017, a meal for 400 students on Republic Day was made using harvest from this field.

The story of this school is incredible in many ways and exemplary of the fact that with some guidance, our youth can do remarkable things and find meaning in their lives. The students and teachers had been dealing with serious issues and the school became the hub for social change in that locality.

The successful aqua-farming project demonstrated by the students became an inspiration for an entire village. At present, there are around 292 ponds in the roughly 300 houses in Vithura. The region has vibrant tourism potential with many hotels and resorts operating and the yield from these ponds is much in demand. The student cadets have not only transformed their own sphere of activities but have also benefited an entire village.

Anver and the cadets have also designed the Bhakshya Suraksha, Manava Raksha (Secure Food, Save Humanity) project. The four components of this project are as follows:

- One Paddy, One Fish (followed by Kuttikulathile Matsyakrushi, i.e., aqua-farming in micro ponds)
- Kuttikk vilavedukkan kutti thengu (little coconut tree for little ones to harvest)
- Zero-budget spiritual farming (micro-farming in grow bags using natural manure like dung of indigenous cows)
- Heritage garden (cultivating indigenous tubers)

This project won the top prize in the Best Innovation category at the Bala Krishi Sasthra Congress organised by the

Centre for Innovation in Science and Social Action (CISSA). The project was also showcased at the World Agriculture Congress held at Tokyo in 2016.

A proud Anver says,

When SPC was started in the school, we were looking at a maximum of one or two students getting A+ in all subjects at the board examinations. Ever since SPC was introduced, there has been a steady improvement in the discipline and academic performance of students. Out of twenty-six students from the school who secured A+ in all subjects in 2018, twenty-one were SPCs. This became twenty-nine out of thirty-five in 2019.

The momentum created by the agriculture project did wonders to the children. It unleashed their urge to innovate. The SPC unit in Vithura rolled out a stream of innovative projects, training the children in sectors that touch all aspects of a common man's life.

A skill hub established for eighty-eight cadets brings out an entire spectrum of products from utility bags made out of newspaper to homemade cakes for Christmas. Twenty boys are engaged in the LED lamp assembling unit, while twins Arathy and Arya Lakshmi are leading a group in handling saplings. The skill hub ensures that students are adept in at least two skills by the time they complete the course and pass out of school.

The search for new and innovative concepts keeps teachers and students moving along. An example is the medicinal garden with the child-friendly police station at Vithura where around eighty plants are grown. Here, the children have done a wonderful job of using modern technology. They prepared a QR code-based recognition and information system for every plant in the garden.

The SPC at Vithura also runs a radio club with specially designed audio booths inside the school. In 2019, the school trained twenty-five RJs. The little RJs have their ten minutes from 1.30 p.m. on Mondays, Wednesdays and Thursdays to do short programmes. They share news, songs and stories.

The SPC unit is also working on organising regular thirty-minute talk shows with a panel of children taking up issues of their interest with local social and political leaders as well as teachers.

When Anver joined the school as an English teacher in 2015, he had been the youngest among the faculty. He was very unsure of what to do about the problems he observed in the school. But the SPC project opened a window of opportunities for him, letting him channel his students' energies to reach amazing levels of creativity and innovation that went beyond the four walls of the classroom.

'I will still not say this is the best the school can produce; yes, it is better than old times, but we can go further. There is a lot more to be done,' says Anver happily.

11

Success Story 6
Designs of an Agonised Mind

When Aslam was in Class V, he started experiencing severe headaches. He was studying in a private CBSE school at the time. A local doctor had wrongly diagnosed his headaches as meningitis and prescribed medicines accordingly. Later, he was diagnosed with Hepatitis A and had to undergo many months of treatment before he could somewhat regain his health.

His medication had side effects and the extended use of antibiotics led Aslam to gain a lot of weight. Initially, he did not think about it as he kept himself busy with hobbies. He loved sketching and drawing machines as they fascinated him. He was eager to recover and return to school so he could show his works to his friends. Little did he know that things were going to be different in school.

He showed his drawings to his classmates and friends when he returned, but he did not get the reaction he had expected.

Instead of cheering him on, they were mean and made fun of his weight. Aslam was subjected to body shaming and made fun of for a condition that was not in his control.

Unfortunately, the practice of humiliating a person for being too thin or too fat is normalised in the world today. Nevertheless, it remains problematic. Body shaming can have lasting effects on the mental health of the person being subjected to it. When a person is subjected to bullying and psychological harassment, victims often slip into a shell and find fault in themselves. The bully manages to convince the victim that they are inadequate and deserve this treatment. This leads to feelings of self-doubt, shame, lack of confidence and depression. Social media has further cemented toxic ideas of how a person should look like.

For a young boy like Aslam, this had devastating effects on his psyche. He felt insecure and lost. Although his teachers appreciated his talents, the constant bullying by his classmates about his weight affected him badly. He would cry all the time. When he tried to complain to his teachers, it led to more intense harassment.

'I was required to complete other's projects for them and help them to cheat in examinations or else I'd get beaten up,' recalls Aslam. Scared and introverted, Aslam withdrew further into himself and obliged every demand placed before him to escape being further victimised.

During one of the PTA meetings, his mother took Aslam's younger brother along. Aslam was very proud to show the beaming three-year-old his classroom. The boys were walking along the first-floor corridor when the bully gang caught up with them. They started heckling the little one and tried to push him over. 'I grabbed my brother and ran towards the auditorium, which was on the fourth floor of another building, to escape from them.' This constant bullying had shattered Aslam so much that he had lost all his confidence.

During another PTA meet, Aslam's teacher thought of making the event more interactive with quizzes and performances for parents. Aslam was chosen to propose the vote of thanks. Thrilled at the opportunity, the young boy prepared a speech, rehearsed it a hundred times and yet, got stuck at the first line when the actual hour came to deliver it. 'I went blank and told my teacher that I felt dizzy.' Aslam was asked to go back to the seat and another boy delivered the speech. He was laughed at and harassed for this as well.

When the bullying became unbearable and no recourse was found, his parents decided to shift Aslam to GHSS Kallar where his mother was a teacher. Immediately, Aslam wanted to be part of SPC.

Joining the SPC and being in an enabling environment after being bullied for so long helped Aslam heal from his trauma. No one here body shamed or made fun of him. This brought out the best in Aslam. He soon became the platoon commander and the parade commander. He oversaw the first platoon during their passing out parade. 'I think I am the only cadet to have participated in two consecutive summer camps and passing out parades as part of two different platoons.'

His enthusiasm for the project kept growing by the day.

'Even after he passed out as an SPC, he used to turn up at the district summer camps. Nothing could keep him away from the camps. He used to come on his own,' remembered S.R. Suresh Babu, an SPC officer. Aslam used to volunteer as a camp officer and took up various activities till he joined an engineering college for graduation.

SPC not only gave Aslam the confidence to stand up and face the adversities, but also provided a channel to explore his creativity. He learnt to respect himself and be confident in who he was. He strived to become the best version of himself. He made two documentaries, *SPC: The Neo Eon* and *Mrutasanjeevani Mruthiyilekko? (Is the elixir of immortality approaching its own death?)* He did most of the work for a third one titled *Man Slayer*, a documentary on addiction and substance abuse, but could not complete it before he left the school.

The energy that SPC provided stood in good stead for Aslam as he moved to MES College of Engineering, Kuttippuram to pursue a degree in electronics and communication. SPC taught him to open up and reach out. He joined the Innovation and Entrepreneurship Development Cell (IEDC), an independent body under the Kerala Start-up Mission.

> There exists a gap between students and industry as students lack proper industrial exposure or training and what we learn from colleges is only basic knowledge. To mitigate that, I proposed a plan to recruit interested students to a talent pool based on their interests including designing, content creation, content writing, data analytics and tech support and to give them training through skill development programmes.

Aslam is also the design student representative for Malabar Hub in the Kerala Chapter of the Institute of Electrical and Electronic Engineers (IEEE). He was the designer for IEEE

PES Day 2020 as well. He has come a long way from the chubby boy who was pushed around by bullies. He emerged as a leader, thanks to SPC. Aslam now gets invited as a speaker at IEEE events and webinars.

12

Success Story 7
I Am More Than a Stereotype

Amitha Fathima.

When a classmate said that her name sounded like that of a 'terrorist', she was jolted and could not get over such a careless comment about who she was and the religion she identified with.

Amitha realised that all the talks about Islamophobia in the contemporary world were real and that she was being subjected to the same hatred and prejudices Muslim communities across the world face, a situation that she probably never thought would play out in her life. Amitha had done her entire schooling at Muslim Higher Secondary School, Erattupetta before moving to St Anne's in Kottayam for Class XI.

Muslim HSS Erattupetta has an illustrious history. It was a daring decision by seven leading Muslim personalities in the region to start a school for Muslim girls in the rural area of Kottayam in the 1950s as formal education for women among Muslim communities was still much of a foreign and unwelcome idea. They challenged this and stood up for the right of education for girls. P.P. Ummer Koya, the then Minister for Public Works, laid the foundation stone for the school on 21 June 1964, and since then, hundreds of Muslim girls from the area have been able to receive formal education.

Amitha grew up within this rich legacy. She was aware of her Muslim identity and the fact that she was among the many Muslim women who were privileged to have received formal education owing to the efforts of some visionary thinkers and supporters of women's rights.

Never had Amitha thought that the popular stereotype of all Muslims being involved in terrorist activities would be used against her by children who probably did not even realise the gravity of what they said.

But despite the hurt that Amitha experienced, she did not want reductive ideas about her or her schoolmates to be the only thing that defined her.

Since Amitha was also a student police cadet, she decided that she could not be casual about this. From that day onwards, Amitha made an extra effort to engage with the girl who made the insensitive remark. Amitha spoke to her about everything—from herself to what she thought of the nation and the work she had been doing as a cadet.

Soon, she became friends with her and was happy that the girl who made a negative comment about her religious identity was able to see that there was so much more to her as a person, as a citizen and as a regular girl her age.

When Amitha was still at Muslim HSS, Ansar Ali, the CPO, told all his students, 'Life may not always present us with favourable conditions. But success lies in trying to change the existing situation into a favourable one for yourself.' This advice always stayed with Amitha. She reminisces:

> I could have continued in Muslim HSS for my Classes XI and XII. The school was close to my home, I had been in the school all my life and I knew the teachers and students there. It was my comfort zone. But my parents and teachers encouraged me when I thought of going to Kottayam and joining St. Anne's Girls Higher Secondary School. It was a challenge and I wanted to take it.

As a girl typically dressed in the traditional Muslim attire with a headscarf, Amitha is equally at ease wearing khakis on the parade ground. Her parents were her greatest support in redefining her identity.

> Once I asked my father about a father writing letters to daughter after I heard a bit about that at school. Next day, he brought me the book by Jawaharlal Nehru. He was that alert. The case is the same with my mother. She could not do much because of her orthodox background and I always felt that she is realising her childhood dreams through me.

Amitha's mother, Mumtaz, defended her daughter's choice of wearing khakis during the parade within the extended family. She told them that Amitha must change with the times, and she knew that her decision for her daughter was right as she has now become a role model for other girls in the community who aim to be like her. 'I feel really proud knowing that other girls in our community are treating my girl as a role model,' said Amitha's mother. Mumtaz realises that she has achieved her goal of making her daughter self-reliant and confident of herself. Amitha's increased social responsibility and her commitment towards the society has also boosted Mumtaz's conviction in the project.

Amitha's engagement with SPC helped her develop a balanced perspective about society and life that went beyond the communal angles and religious identities. She got numerous opportunities to understand herself better. For instance, cadets are required to present an analysis of news reports every Saturday. This helped Amita hone her public-speaking skills and analytical abilities. She immensely enjoys public speaking.

For Amitha, the SPC community was like her extended family. She says,

> CPO Ali Sir and Additional CPO Salama Jacob were great support to me while I was a cadet. I was much attached to my grandfather who died while I was a cadet. Salama Ma'am held me close to her while breaking this news to me and said you should not cry; you are a student police cadet. Those words worked like magic on me and helped me get over the grief. I would have faltered if it was not for SPC at that point.

Since it was introduced, the SPC project has been a changemaker for the youth in Kerala. They have begun to explore a world beyond their immediate environment and academics and started adopting a holistic approach towards civic life. Amitha Fathima is one of the many shining faces that emerge from the frame that SPC has built.

Amitha's tenure with SPC taught her that it was not about the forty-four cadets who marched under the sun along with her. It was about forty-four families, their neighbourhood and everyone who lived in that space. As a science student, she has the option of pursuing a career in the medical field as a doctor or a nurse. Civil service is also within her spectrum of goals right now. But underneath all these goals, her vision remains crystal clear. 'I want to give back to the nation that has given birth to me. SPC gave me that vision and that is guiding me now, in whichever profession I choose.'

This clarity gives her the courage and conviction to analyse and go deep into the concept of religion as an integral part of her life and community space.

13

Success Story 8
Hands to Serve and a Heart to Love

Mini Mathew is the physical education teacher at the Holy Family High School, Parampuzha. As a natural athlete with a never-say-die attitude, she always wants to finish her run and win it. She has a fire in her spirit that is obvious when you see her.

Mini, a mother of three children and wife to a retired higher secondary school teacher, had a tough childhood marked with hunger and penury. She realised the agony of being denied chances in life. So, when she became a teacher, Mini tried to see the reality from the side of the children. She empathised with the needy and tried to hold their hands to pull them out of the corners life had pushed them to.

Her school was established way back in 1911 in a poor neighbourhood. The area is low on the social scale and the children growing up there were exposed to the rampant use of narcotic drugs.

My first experience with the severity of the issue was when I tried to check out why one of my students was regularly missing from the class. Much to our shock, we found him locked himself up in the bathroom in his house with intense withdrawal symptoms. Even the house was in a pathetic condition. So, we took the initiative to rebuild the home and also to rehabilitate the boy.

Mini Mathew took up the crusade against narcotics abuse among youth. There was not much she could do to check the prevalence of drugs in the region, which had by then become a hub for narcotic sales and use. She, along with Headmistress Mariamma K.V., could only ensure that no sale of narcotic drugs took place within and around the school premises. But the children continued to be vulnerable.

Mini tried to engage the police officials with whom she had contact through the SPC project and initiated raids in surrounding neighbourhoods. She did ruffle some feathers and break some networks as was evident when there were concerted efforts to target her personally. A couple of cases were registered against her alleging her involvement in organ trade.

However, Mini is not the one to be discouraged. With support from the police officers in the district and colleagues at school, she is fighting the cases legally.

Mini is one of those persons who puts the welfare of others over her own needs. This was demonstrated when she stepped forward to donate her kidney to Remya, a woman from a low-income background in Kottarakkara. She came to know about the woman through the Kidney Foundation of India, headed by Father David Chirammel. The foundation is a one-of-a-kind NGO that facilitates and supports persons with renal failure as well as spreads awareness on organ donation.

Mini Mathew, then Additional CPO, was felicitated at the SPC Annual Summer Camp in 2014 for her humanitarian services through voluntary donation of her kidney. In her acceptance speech at the function, she motivated the cadets by expressing her willingness to donate a part of her liver too, which she can do after two years of her kidney operation.

In her speech, she requested the police officers, especially P. Vijayan, to amend the anti-narcotics act and make the punishment for possession of narcotics more stringent. 'I have watched one of my students go through excruciating pain during rehabilitation. I want to save him and many others from this traumatic situation,' Mini said.

Mini has also been at the forefront in the effort to reach out to the people who need support. She helped her student, Jeena, who was very studious till Class VIII, but stopped coming to school after her leg was amputated due to leukaemia. Mini took the initiative to bring her back to normal life. During weekends, she took her classmates to visit her at home.

'When we first arrived there, she was very withdrawn. She would not even raise her eyes from the phone in her hands. Slowly, we managed to break her silence and get warm responses.' Then, Mini Mathew took the initiative to raise funds under the Friends@Home project of SPC and bought a wheelchair for her. The young girl has now completed her schooling and is now a graduation student at K.E. College, Mannanam.

The fire that started in her when she had visited a home during her initial years as part of the team conducting electoral enumeration is still aflame. During her visit, she spotted a woman who was locked up in her home because her husband had accused her of being promiscuous. Mini did not think much before contacting the police and social welfare officials to sort out the issue and liberate the woman from domestic violence. Mini retains the eye to spot a person in pain during her social engagements.

As a teacher, she passes on that quality to her students too. In 2016, she came across a platform that accepts hair donations for making wigs for cancer patients. 'Mothers of children at school were reeling under shame like this then. So, I contacted the agencies that collect hair and make wigs. They said they needed more volunteers. Children were not willing to donate at first, but I stepped forward. I did not have the minimum length, but I asked to close crop my hair.'

Her action was so inspiring that eleven others followed suit. This included seven cadets, two teachers, one peon and her daughter. Since then, Mini has donated her hair two more times.

Through her efforts, Mini keeps inspiring hundreds of children to emerge as changemakers in their own respective social circles.

14

Success Story 9
Be the Change, Make the Change

As she sat down in full uniform and waiting for the online chat room to open, the words of Inspector General of Police P. Vijayan, who is in charge of SPC, kept ringing in Aadiya's ears. 'You are one of the five cadets who will be the face of this project. Do your best.'

Aadiya Silia was one among the cadets selected to interact with Henry F. De Sio Jr., author, international keynote speaker, campaign and innovation strategist and chief operating officer at the United Nations Foundation. These cadets were representing 1,00,000 young changemakers comprising present and former student police cadets. The programme was organised on 21 May 2020.

'I was a little nervous but sure that I would do give my best to stand up to the honour bestowed upon me.' And Aadiya proved herself right. She stood out among the participants and captured the attention of Henry when the cadets were given time to introduce themselves. At the end of the online interaction, which was telecast on web channels across the world, the cadets were given a chance to raise one more question and Aadiya was the first to raise her hand.

She confidently spoke about the 'Yes We Can!' campaign that Henry had designed as Barack Obama's campaign head during his pre-election strategy. She asked why youth from across the world cannot establish a network to counter the pandemic. To this, Henry responded by saying every person has the ability to initiate a change and that the youth is wired for it through networks and connections, thus welcoming Aadiya's question.

Aadiya studied at Calicut University Campus till Class VII. She was drawn towards theatre, public speaking, debating and participating in seminars. There were a couple of teachers in her neighbourhood who worked in the M.V. Higher Secondary School at Ariyannur. They suggested Aadiya move to their school.

The first thing that Aadiya noticed on joining her new school was SPC members doing their parades and other civic duties in and around the school. For someone who had her ambition set on becoming a police officer, the opportunity was irresistible. She took the test and passed it.

During the pandemic in 2020, the SPC provided multiple opportunities to cadets for service to others, thus unleashing the changemaking spirit in Aadiya. She recollects that March to May 2020 were the best three months of her life.

The SPC project gave regular tasks to the cadets to keep them engaged throughout the day and remain positive. The list started with yoga and proceeded to providing water for birds and stray animals, reading, gardening and connecting with each other through calls. She remembers witnessing peacocks and monkeys coming out of the nearby forest area and roaming freely. 'Initially, I was very angry that the monkeys were taking mangoes from our trees. But then I realised this is originally their space. Now that we have been locked up, they are reclaiming their space.'

Aadiya is an inherently compassionate person and her engagement with the SPC brought this fact to the fore. During the lockdown, hygiene protocol was stressed upon. Whenever she or other students stepped out to distribute food, the teachers wanted them to strictly follow the COVID-19 prevention protocol of wearing masks and washing hands regularly. Aadiya decided to stitch a three-layer cloth mask that could be reused instead of a single-use mask that needed to be discarded. 'I felt that this particular task was meant just for me,' she remarked retrospectively. She decided to make many more to distribute for free.

Just as she was stepping out of her home with a hundred hand-made masks for policemen on duty, her grandmother called her. 'Look, they are working under scorching sun, take this buttermilk. This must be ten or twelve glasses; give it to them.'

The Calicut University bus stop was 150 metres away from her home. 'I was sure there must be policemen on duty there.' She was right. There were six policemen there. Aadiya says that she was confident that they would not rebuke her for stepping out during lockdown because of her SPC uniform.

Aadiya remembers the police personnel were drenched in sweat. The sub-inspector was leaning against the police jeep.

He was busy, yet he smiled and signalled her to come closer. 'I wanted to give them a salute, but I was carrying the bowl of buttermilk in one hand and the masks in another. I stood in attention before them.'

The sub-inspector asked why she was out on the road at that hour.

'Sir, I came to hand over these masks to you and your team. This is the SPC team's contribution to what you are doing for us.'

He looked at Aadiya in amazement. His look gave her courage and inspiration.

'Sir, this is buttermilk my grandmother asked me to share with you.'

She could see the officer's and his team's expression change from amazement to admiration. He read her name on the uniform—Aadiya Silia, Student Police Cadet.

'Sir, we learn to serve,' she said with pride.

Before leaving, Aadiya promised the officer and his team that she would be there every day to provide buttermilk to those on duty. Aadiya missed only two days in the next two-and-a-half months.

Another task that the SPC directorate gave to cadets was to create videos to raise awareness around safety protocols for COVID-19 to be shared on social media. Aadiya made around thirty such videos to be posted on social media to fulfil the tasks assigned to her and seventy more videos on her own accord.

She did not stop at that. Every day, the cadets were given an online class on a variety of subjects. She would then make a video of her own, trying to explain what she had learnt in those sessions and share it with her teachers. 'When my teachers approve of what I have created, I achieve two things. One, I am clearer about what I have learnt and two, I can pass on that information to those who are not part of the SPC project.' Till date, she has made about twenty such videos.

'The concept of changemaking has restructured the world order from a hierarchical one to "everyone-is-a-changemaker" mode. Empathy-based ethics, where people are making decisions for the good of all, is the new societal imperative,' said Henry during the interaction he had with the cadets.

'I still hear those words within me,' says Aadiya. And she lives by those words. Every day. Every hour.

15

Success Story 10
The Elixir of Life

Anshida loved rings. She was constantly looking for simple designs but realised that buying a gold ring would be too much to ask of her parents. That's why she started collecting what little money she got as gifts during special occasions.

The money was kept in an envelope, which she would check every day. She would count it and put it back. It was very special for her. There was some maintenance work underway at her home and she knew that her family needed the money, but they did not ask her for her savings. They all knew her love for rings and how long she had been collecting bit by bit for one.

During maintenance work, Anshida's family moved into the house of her father's brother, two houses away from theirs. They were all staying in 6 Cent Colony, a name that the neighbourhood had acquired owing to its houses being supposedly built with just six cents.

One day, Anshida noticed an auto-rickshaw driving up the unpaved road to the end of the colony. Being an inquisitive child, she checked it out. The auto-rickshaw was carrying water to the house of Nadukudi Kunjen and his wife, Thanka.

Anshida knew the aged couple. She used to visit them. Kunjen was fully blind and Thanka had partially impaired vision. They lived in a rickety house with basic facilities. Almost every house in the colony had a well, but the one at Kunjen's place had dried up.

'There was a common panchayat well, but people mostly used it to dump garbage,' says Saleena Karuvathodikkal, a panchayat ward member. The auto-rickshaw charged ₹100 for one trip, which was way beyond the means of eighty-year-old Kunjen and his seventy-year-old wife. They lived out of a meagre pension they had. Anshida knew this.

Her training at SPC had taught her that there were no problems without solutions. She discussed the issue with her parents and uncle. A pipe could be laid to connect the old couple's house to the nearest source of water. It would take around 300 metres of PVC pipes and a storage tank.

The residents of the colony managed to find someone to sponsor the storage tank, but the pipe needed to be purchased. It had to be crowdfunded. The first contribution took everyone by surprise.

It was Anshida. She brought out the envelope in which she had been saving money to buy a gold ring for herself. She had saved exactly ₹3,000. She gave it all. The remaining funds (around ₹5,000) flowed in shortly after.

'This little one is our protector,' said Kunjen, holding Anshida's hand, his sightless eyes welling up. Both Kunjen and Thanka realised that what Anshida hadn't just provided them a water pipeline, it was a lifeline.

But Anshida remained nonchalant about it all. 'I have known them for long and it was natural for me to respond like that.' Growing up watching her father, Kummali Mujeeb, a truck driver, helping others, Anshida was natural indeed. But her SPC membership gave her enough avenues to explore and help those in need. Kunjettan, as she called Kunjen, was right there before her.

When the nation went into lockdown, those like Kunjen and Thanka were the first to be hit. They were like the people IG Vijayan saw sleeping on the footpath. On that day, Vijayan had been returning after attending a meeting convened to discuss how to effectively implement the lockdown. Looking at the people asleep on the pavement, Vijayan wondered from where they would get their next meal.

It was that thought that led to one of the most extraordinary programmes implemented during the pandemic-induced lockdown. The Feed A Stomach campaign was launched across the state and as instructed by the chief minister, state-run community kitchens were set up. Food packets from these kitchens did not reach just the homeless, but also those who were stranded midway in travel, students in hostels, patients and their bystanders in hospitals, guest labourers who came from different parts of the country and could not return and the tribal communities who remained in the peripheries of society.

What started off as a small step inside the limits of the capital city, Thiruvananthapuram, was extended to all nine police districts of the state. Food prepared in around twenty-four kitchens and Feed A Stomach centres was distributed to beneficiaries identified through police and community networks.

By the end of May 2021, as many as 9,00,452 food packets were distributed. Along with this, food material kits, which are enough for a five-member family for five days, were distributed to 39,046 families. Young and vibrant kids like Anshida chipped in by contributing through voluntary service and donations to neighbourhood community kitchens run by local self-government bodies.

Lavana Nazeer, a fellow cadet of Anshida, says,

We distributed nearly 30 such food kits to the Scheduled Tribe Colony. We used to distribute clothes and food to the Mancheri Colony nearby, where seventy-odd tribal families live. Mostly members from tribes like Cholanayikkars or Kattunayakan live there. However, we are often stopped by police warning us about Maoist presence there. Still, we go over when it is safe and give material to them.

The second wave of pandemic was harsher. The Feed A Stomach programme had been stopped once the restrictions were relaxed, but the second wave surged in soon after. The idea of a community kitchen was not practical as the new variant was more contagious. No such risk could be taken, especially one involving the cadets.

But then the crisis provided a chance to reinvent strategies. The cadets were among the first responders during the second wave of the pandemic to collect packed food and distribute them efficiently. During the first week itself, more than 20,000 food packets were distributed among the homeless and medical assistance was provided to the needy in different districts of Kerala.

On her part, Anshida returned to Kunjen and Thanka with kits of vegetables and provisions. She got support from her neighbour, Poonkuzhi Mustafah, to buy all that the couple needed and went over to give it to them. For her, lessons learnt at SPC have become a way of life. It is something she will always cherish.

16

Success Story 11
Words Beyond Silence

The ways in which student police cadets reach out to society are amazing. Since its inception, the programme has been designed to nurture leadership qualities in very young minds. Students are trained to respond to extraordinary situations through innovative engagements.

Kutty Desk—which means 'little desk'—was one such avenue for the children. This was an innovative programme that cadets and a child-oriented state-run programme called Our Responsibility to Children (ORC) initiated during the pandemic period. This was probably a one-of-its-kind initiative where children were trained to provide telephonic guidance to their peers on sanitation and personal hygiene during lockdown.

The idea of providing telephonic guidance started with ten students under the ORC programme in Kollam. Later, it was extended across the state. Karthika Krishnan, district coordinator of ORC for Kollam, says:

We collected the numbers from where distress calls were made from the District Medical Office and police stations. Children were trained to call these numbers and talk to kids in the family about keeping a positive outlook and engaging in productive activities like kitchen gardening instead of spending too much time on mobile phones. Right from the beginning, we made it clear that these children were not doing counselling, but helping their peers locked up at home in handling the situation by sharing the official guidelines.

The programme, which was started in April 2020, operated in full swing till August in that year. It was revived during the second wave. More than 200 children from SPC and ORC were selected and trained to handle the calls and between them, they contacted around 20,000 children over the phone in this period.

Even though the children were trained to pass on very general information regarding personal hygiene and positivity, there were calls when they had to face unexpected responses. Farsana S., who was waiting for her Class XII board examination results when she was a part of Kutty Desk, had one such experience.

She was a student at GHSS Chithara in Thiruvananthapuram Rural. The practice was to pool the numbers collected from the District Medical Office and police stations and distribute them among Kutty Desk volunteers.

One such call had Farsana conversing with a boy. She recalls the incident saying,

He sounded very low right from the beginning. I assumed that it might be because of not being able to be with friends or go to school. So, after sharing the basic information, I probed a little further and tried to cheer him up.

But what the boy shared was not what Farsana had expected. The boy had been deeply attached to his grandfather. They had spent a lot of time together before the pandemic broke out. He was a single child and his parents were busy with their work. The child and grandfather had shared stories, made paintings and played games together. During the lockdown, the grandfather died of age-related ailments, leaving the boy in intense trauma.

> I did not know what to say or how to respond. For a while, I remained silent and let him talk and cry. I was more of a listener as I felt the boy needed someone to release his pent-up trauma and grief.

An undergrad student of English literature at the historic University College, Trivandrum — one of the oldest colleges in the country—Farsana now realises how important her silence was back then. Giving companionship to those in grief and in bereavement is an alien concept in our society. The grief phase is often softened by rituals and ceremonies related to death and cremation. But informed support with scientifically solid awareness is also needed. This gap was exposed during the pandemic when people had to let go of all the rituals, including those connected to death.

That was behind the long silence that Farsana had to maintain while the boy opened up his bag of sorrow to her. And she was not alone in this. Many more were in varying states of disorientation as they could not handle the process of grieving in the changed situation. This accentuated the need to have a proper, scientifically designed programme to support those in grief and bereavement. The first to respond to this trigger was Mission Better Tomorrow, a not-for-profit organisation and a knowledge partner for the SPC programme. Mission Better Tomorrow has a legacy of fifteen years of work in empowering young people through education and capacity building.

Mission Better Tomorrow partnered with the Institute of Palliative Medicine (IPM), a WHO Collaborating Centre for Community Participation in Palliative Care and Long-term Care and the Death Literacy Institute (DLI), Australia, to address this sensitive issue. The result was the Bereavement Companionship Programme, a first-of-its-kind initiative in India.

The response to the programme was very encouraging. People readily came forward to learn more about how to provide bereavement companionship. To date, Mission Better Tomorrow, along with IPM and DLI, has conducted seven online batches, each spread over fifteen hours in three days. This included two international batches comprising participants from Bangladesh and Thailand.

After a couple of batches, teams of young people gathered at IPM to design a proper training manual for the programme. The curriculum covered sessions on 'knowing oneself', 'learning from previous death experiences' and 'better communication skills' along with familiarisation with theories on handling grief and bereavement. The programme also has an entire session dedicated to knowing how grief impacts children of different age groups.

The highlight of the Bereavement Companionship Programme is an online course operated by Mission Better

Tomorrow, IPM and DLI exclusively for participants from Bangladesh. This course had the Palliative Care Society of Bangladesh (PCSB) and Phoenix Wellness Centre, Bangladesh too as partners.

Commenting on the programme, Prof. Dr Nezamuddin Ahmad, Founder Director of PCSB, said that even though providing companionship to bereaved ones is an integral component of the social and religious matrix of Bangladeshi society, the pandemic changed it all. They were totally unprepared to handle social isolation while grieving for the dead or dying, which had a long-lasting impact on the mental health of society in general.

When Farsana dialled the number of the boy randomly chosen from the list shared by the group formed at Kutty Desk, she had not been aware of any of these complexities and social dilemmas. She never knew the trauma of one of the participants in the Bangladeshi session, a mother of two, whose elder son had been raped and murdered the year before and was facing difficulties in dealing with the psychological issues of the younger son. She knew absolutely nothing about internationally accepted models like the TEAR model and Tonkin model of grief. But she responded in a way that came naturally to her when encountered with a young boy shattered by bereavement grief.

Her response highlighted the need to initiate a proper and scientifically-based programme. Enterprising young minds who respond to social stimuli are the harbingers of change in our society. Farsana, though unintentionally, became one herself.

SECTION III
Praise for SPC

17

No Going Back

Muhammad Yunus
Nobel Peace Laureate 2006
Founder, Grameen Bank, The Bank for the Poor

The extent of damage that the pandemic caused the world is difficult to grasp. However, despite the damage, it offered us an unparalleled opportunity.

Right now, the big question that we must answer is: do we take the world back to pre-COVID-19 days? Or do we redesign the world? The decision is entirely ours.

COVID-19 changed the context and calculus of the world. It has opened audacious possibilities that never existed before. Suddenly we are at the tabula rasa. We can go in any direction we want. What an unbelievable freedom of choice!

But before that we must agree on what kind of economy we want. First and foremost, we have to agree that the economy is a means. It facilitates us to reach the goals set by us. It should not behave like a death trap designed by some divine power to punish us. We should not forget for a moment that it is a tool made by us. We must keep on designing and redesigning it until we arrive at the highest level of collective happiness.

If at any point we feel that it is not taking us where we want to go, we immediately know that there is something wrong with the hardware or software that we are currently using. All we need to do is to fix it. There is no excuse. Whether it's about building a world with net-zero carbon emissions, zero unemployment or no concentration of wealth, we have to simply build the right machinery to facilitate the same. We have the power. When human beings set their mind to get something done, they just do it. Nothing is impossible.

The most exciting news is that the COVID-19 crisis offers us almost limitless opportunities to make a fresh start. But the redesign must be based on social and environmental consciousness.

One simple unanimous global decision will help us tremendously: the decision that we don't want to go back to where we came from. We don't want to jump into the same frying pan in the name of recovery.

We should not even call it a 'recovery' programme. To make our purpose clear, we may call it a 'reconstruction' programme. Businesses will be made to play a key role to make it happen. The point of departure for the post-COVID-19 reconstruction programme must be done by putting social and environmental consciousness firmly at the centre stage for all decision-making. Governments must guarantee that not a single penny shall be offered to anyone unless the government is sure that it will foster maximum social and environmental benefit to society compared to all other options.

We must start with 'reconstruction' packages for plans driven by social consciousness and disregard the naysayers. Strong cases will be made to derail the new initiatives by saying these are untested policies. When we proposed that the Olympics be designed as social businesses, opponents made the same arguments. Now the Paris 2024 Summer Olympics are being designed that way with great enthusiasm. The time for bold, dynamic change is NOW.

In this comprehensive reconstruction plan, I propose to give the central role to a new form of business called social business. It is a business created solely for solving people's problems, without no focus on personal profit. After the original investment is met, all subsequent profits are ploughed back into the business.

Governments will have many opportunities to encourage, prioritise and open spaces for social businesses to undertake major redesigning responsibilities. At the same time, governments must launch their own programmes, such as taking care of the destitute and the unemployed through traditional welfare programmes, offering healthcare, reviving all essential services and supporting all types of businesses where social business options are slow to come forward.

To speed up the entry of social businesses, governments can create social business venture capital funds, centrally and locally, by encouraging the private sector, foundations, financial institutions and investment funds, to contribute or become social businesses themselves or take in social business partners.

Under the rebuilding programme, governments can finance social businesses to buy companies or tie-up with needy companies to transform them into social businesses. Central banks can allow social businesses to receive funds from financial institutions to invest in the stock market.

There will be so many opportunities arising from the rebuilding process; governments should involve as many social business actors as possible.

So, who are the social business investors? Where do we find them?

They are everywhere. We don't see them because our current economic textbooks don't recognise their existence. As a result, our eyes are not trained to see them. Only nowadays are economics courses including discussions on topics like social business, entrepreneurship, impact investment and non-profit organisations as side issues inspired by the global admiration for Grameen Bank and microcredit.

As long as economics remains a science for profit maximisation, we cannot rely entirely on it for a reconstruction programme based on social and environmental consciousness. The whole strategy would be to enlarge the proportion of social business as the economy develops. Its success will be visible when it grows into a larger percentage of the economy, but there will also be rapid growth in the number of entrepreneurs where the same entrepreneurs are doing both types of businesses. This will signal the beginning of a social- and environmental-consciousness-driven economy.

As soon as government policy starts recognising social business entrepreneurs and investors, such individuals will come forward enthusiastically to play the role demanded by the historical opportunity. Social business entrepreneurs are not members of a small do-gooder community. This is a significant global ecosystem that includes giant multinational companies, big social business funds, many talented CEOs, corporate bodies, foundations and trusts with many years of experience who will be valuable in addressing the current social and economic crises.

We must remember that people are born as entrepreneurs—not job seekers. The reconstruction programme must break down the traditional division of work between citizens and the government. It is taken for granted that the citizens' role is to take care of their families and pay taxes while it is the responsibility of the government—and to a limited extent, the non-profit sector—to take care of all collective problems like climate, jobs, healthcare, education, water and so on. Reconstruction programmes should break this wall of separation and encourage all citizens to come forward and show their talent as problem-solvers by creating social businesses. Their strength is not in the size of their initiatives but in their number. Each small initiative multiplied by a big number results in significant national action.

A problem that social business entrepreneurs can immediately address is that of unemployment by building businesses that create jobs. They can also open up the option of transforming the unemployed into entrepreneurs. Social businesses can engage in improving the current health infrastructure in collaboration with the government system.

The desperation and urgency of the post-COVID-19 world demands a wake-up call from governments, leading to a surge of activities never seen before. This will be the test of leadership to show how a world can be inspired to be reborn in completely unknown ways—coming from the youths, the middle-aged and the elderly.

However, if we fail to create a socially and environmentally sustainable economy, we will be heading for a catastrophe that is many times worse that what the pandemic showed us. We could hide in our homes from COVID-19, but if we fail to address deteriorating global issues, we will not have any place to hide from Mother Nature and the angry masses around the world.

18

Setting the Tone for a Gender-equal World*

Dr Yasmin Ali Haque
Former UNICEF Representative, India

Let me begin by congratulating the SPC team, the Kerala state police, who have been behind this project and IG Vijayan's commitment to the project. The project itself is an excellent initiative to strengthen engagement with our young people; a very genuine concept that has touched many lives. This book aims to share some of its learnings and possibilities with the public and it is my honour and privilege to be part of this endeavour.

Kerala, now considered one of India's most developed states, shares its title with Himachal Pradesh, with a score of 69 compared to the average 57 of Indian states on the SDG

---

*The author served as 'Representative, India' for UNICEF. The data cited in this chapter has been reviewed and cleared by UNICEF India

India Index of 2018. The state has also done particularly well in achieving good health and well-being, providing quality education and ensuring gender equality, with a commendable literacy rate of 94 per cent, according to the 2011 Census. Out of the 3.4 million children in the state, 88.68 per cent between the ages of five to seventeen years of age are in school, with the opportunity to contribute significantly to the demographic dividend.

Despite its progress, crimes against and involving children have reportedly been on the rise in Kerala. In 2016 alone, out of 817 crimes against children in Kerala, 88 were committed in schools, while 406 were committed in public places. The Kerala State Commission for Protection of Child Rights has revealed that 1,029 children between the ages of fifteen and eighteen and 800 children between the ages of ten and fourteen were victims of sexual harassment. Children spend most of their time in schools; yet, there is presence of drug peddlers, tobacco, pornographic materials and many other harmful substances within the four walls of the school. These children are then exposed to addiction, substance misuse, sexual abuse, exploitation, trafficking, deviant behaviour and crime. Additionally, they face bullying and other emotional and mental forms of abuse by teachers, peers or family members. According to the police, cybercrime and technological addictions are also major issues in the lives of younger children. Children would greatly benefit from opportunities and support in understanding their rights to a life free of violence and abuse to help them realise their full potential.

There remain many areas where a lot more needs to be done, one of them being finding ways to decrease gender-based violence. For example, in the year 2020, an astounding 4,98,531 cases of crimes against women and children were registered in India according to data released from the National Crime Records Bureau, out of which 3,00,000 were against women and the remaining 1,28,531 were against children.

Drug abuse has been one of the most major issues in Kerala, with approximately 3,922 Narcotic Drugs and Psychotropic Substances (NDPS) cases registered in 2021 alone, contributing to 7 per cent of India's overall NDPS cases in 2021. Approximately 22,000 lives were lost in the country last year due to addiction-induced depression or overdose; however, the threat only keeps growing, throwing more and more lives at risk. Sensing the increasing danger, SPC started the Vimukthi campaign, which is an anti-narcotics movement focused on raising awareness on the seriousness of substance abuse and educating the public of Kerala. Vimukthi has set up de-addiction centres in fourteen districts of Kerala and hospitals and counselling centres in Kochi, Kozhikode and Thiruvananthapuram. All these are aimed at battling the impending danger of drug abuse faced by society. Today, the Vimukthi campaign has evolved into a full-fledged NGO operating state-wide along with others organisations like Kudumbasree, the NSS and the Excise Department of Kerala. It is commendable that SPC allowed Vimukthi to grow into such a large movement beyond SPC itself. This has helped Vimukthi to change the mindset and views of the public—something that would not have been possible if its scope was limited. In collaboration with other well-known and well-intentioned organisations supporting it in its journey to battle substance abuse nationwide, the Vimukthi movement will make major breakthroughs in the future, and I look forward to seeing that day soon.

Women continue to face challenges vis-à-vis ownership over resources, especially land resources, decision-making, mobility and their role in civic society, the parliament and elsewhere. The growth we are currently witnessing in the number of women accessing resources and being empowered is only a fraction of their true potential. These challenges are much greater for adolescent girls; for instance, as per NFHS-4, only 22 per cent of girls aged fifteen to nineteen have the freedom of movement to visit a health facility, marketplace or even go outside their village.

The pandemic exacerbated problems of gender-based violence; in the year 2021 alone, around 20,767 cases of crimes against women and children were registered in Kerala. Of these, 16,418 were against women and the remaining 4,349 were against children. Crimes against children are increasing at an alarming rate, exponentially raising the need for child empowerment and safety.

Various organisations such as the Atma Foundation, the Kerala State Women's Development Corporation Ltd and Sakhi Kerala have taken up this cause, slowly but surely turning the tables, equipping both women and children to stand up for themselves and contribute to society. Within the state, SPC has transformed over 11,000 children into young individuals capable of being the change they wish to see in society, contributing largely to women and child empowerment and playing a major role in boosting the confidence of both the cadets and their families.

I sincerely hope that such positive changes in the women involved with SPC will motivate others in realising their inherent potential leading to a chain reaction and greater progress on this front. While on the subject, it is gratifying to witness active efforts for increased and equitable participation of women in local governance. The Kudumbasree programme for promoting women's entrepreneurship and leadership, private partnerships like She Taxi promoting employment for women and contributing to making public spaces safe and gender-friendly are noteworthy examples, and I hope that SPC will continue to identify more such organisations and associate with them. Another challenge that makes us aspire to do even better, for instance, is the latest National Family Health Survey, which places Kerala among the eight states with a dip in the sex ratio at birth over the past five years.

The state sex ratio reduced to 951 in 2019–20 from 1047 in 2015–16 as per NFHS-5. Sex ratio at birth indicates how a society values girls; globally, girls have higher survival rates at birth but India is one of the few countries where more girls die than boys at birth. This might have its roots in the socialisation that starts with children. This process, which starts at or before birth and continues through adolescence and beyond, tends to enhance the privilege and power of men and boys relative to women and girls and children of all genders. Once, I met someone on a field trip who had not yet tried to see his baby girl because she had been born during a certain phase of the moon, and he believed that it would bring bad luck to the family if he saw the child before she was forty days old. It's high time we get rid of this stigma.

Even in the year 2020, we have certain age-old prejudices impacting our society. Socialisation is different, and girls and boys experience adolescence differently, not to mention the experience of transgender children. Boys tend to experience greater freedom; girls tend to face more limitations to their movement, affecting their work, education, marriage and social relationships. A colleague working for the UN once told me that on wanting to pursue her Master's, her father said, 'Okay, you go, but the required money will come out of your dowry.' By commodifying girls and women, the gender barriers we place on children continue into adulthood and the challenges women face over resources, decision-making and the propensity for violence reflects what starts in childhood. Working women and mothers are constantly juggling the different roles. However, they may not have a supportive family giving them confidence and telling them that their priority must be getting a degree and becoming financially self-sufficient no matter what. It is essential that parents set the tone and give girls and boys the same opportunity to get ahead in life. Maternity benefits are crucial in providing opportunities for women, and that would mean providing space for women to breastfeed their babies and for men and women to bring their kids to crèches if needed. How can we bring that change in role? My late father once asked me, 'What is the longest battle in the world?' After a couple of incorrect guesses, he said, 'It is the battle of the sexes.' The tragedy is that we're in a battle; however, when we talk about equality, equal value and equal opportunity for the sexes, we do not talk about one gender over another. Every child born, whether it is a boy, girl or transgender, has the right to reach their full potential.

Kerala is one of the most progressive states in India; it has spearheaded some of the most promising and interesting women and girl empowerment programmes for over two decades. The government has set aside a total of close to ₹4,000 crores, which is about 18 per cent of the total state plan outlay towards the gender budget for 2020–21. That said, gender is not just about girls and women; gender is the role that the different sexes occupy in society and how that affects their aspirations, opportunities and achievements. It is therefore important that we understand the role of the boy. The general mindset is that a boy or man is caring if he listens to his sister and is respectful to his mother, but after marriage, consulting with his wife on decisions brands him as being under her thumb—this is not acceptable. Another case is the burden boys face when they are expected to be wage earners. They are also expected to be prepared to provide old-age security for their parents. Both are huge burdens. How can we all work together for girls and boys to support their family collectively? We need to give boys and girls, men and women, the opportunity to rise above gender-based prejudices, to assert their roles, and simultaneously focus on making the home and community free of violence against children and women. We have seen an increase in domestic violence and gender-based violence in many communities and societies. When we value girls as much as boys, violence against women will no longer be hidden and the act will bring shame to the perpetrator of violence (and not the girl/women) no matter their sex, ethnicity or position in life.

India has seen various organisations stepping up and contributing to society to reduce the gap between the genders as it exists today. In India, women empowerment and safety is an issue that pioneers such as Raja Ram Mohan Roy and Ishwar Chandra Vidyasagar had spearheaded in the nineteenth century. We now need to accelerate the pace. The first step to such equality is educating the public. Luckily, this is a part of the agenda that SPC implements on a national level by transforming over 4,00,000 girls into changemakers doing their bit to fight the 'battle of the sexes'.

We must work together to model positive gender norms, and I am happy with the contributions SPC has made towards this purpose. We need more boys to be part of the positive-gender-norms movement and through SPC we can easily, consistently and accurately measure variables like completion of education, transition to higher education, employment rates and—one of the biggest challenges we face in India—child marriage. SPC also equips us to look at the conversation in a way that does not restrict the focus to education and career but encourages us to investigate what men and boys in the family can do to help change the gender stereotype. By sharing some household chores and the burden of child care, by being more committed to seeing that the girls can complete their education and by being proactive in mitigating the barriers of equal opportunity at work, each family can contribute a small part to this extensive mission.

UNICEF has been working continuously to help increase children and adolescents' understanding of gender norms and building their skills and agency to challenge prejudices at an early age. These changes need to take place at the level of the family. Are women of the households so entrenched in the expectations of a society in the past that they are now repeating this behaviour for the next generation? The role of agencies like UNICEF and civil society organisations is to develop gender-transformative programmes that tackle the root causes of gender inequality and reshape unequal power relations. We work with young boys and girls, providing incentives for them to be in school in a safe manner and address ignorant mindsets.

We also have an edutainment series called 'Aadha Full', which is targeted at adolescents and addresses a lot of these issues; so far, we have reached about 40 million young people to educate them on critical issues of gender stereotypes and gender-based violence. Therefore, there are so many projects for us to work on with SPC and I am happy that SPC is working on solutions that are open and inclusive.

Since its launch, SPC has come a long way to being a full-fledged organisation scaling up and expanding its boundaries to work on a national basis following the announcement by the Hon'ble Minister of Defence, Rajnath Singh, to introduce SPC to all states in India. I am pleased to follow its journey from the early vision of IG Vijayan to the stature it has now reached under his able guidance and support. Instances of the success of SPC in states of India besides Kerala have already been seen, and this project is one that deserves attention and respect from every nation around the world that wants a civil society.

From the cadet from Andaman and Nicobar who single-handedly uncovered and provided crucial information resulting in the arrest and prosecution of a group engaged in making and selling illicit liquor, to the young girl who helped nab Naxalites due to her observational powers and presence of mind; there are sensational stories all around. Even with mundane tasks like regulating vehicular traffic and educating the public on the importance of wearing helmets and seatbelts while travelling in two- and four-wheelers, respectively, SPC has empowered the youth associated with the programme to contribute more towards society. It has also played a huge role in the progress made on issues of gender equality, women's empowerment, safety of the public and general quality of living. It truly is an honour to be associated with such an organisation and I look forward to all the milestones that our youth of tomorrow will reach as part of SPC to usher in a better future for everyone regardless of their sex, caste, religion or any other distinguishing factors.

19

The World's Largest School Transformation Programme

Manoj Kumar Jha
Founder, Basix Education

It is, perhaps, India's best kept secret: the world's largest school transformation programme, the Student Police Cadets, which originated in Kerala. It was founded by an IPS officer, P. Vijayan. Currently, IG Vijayan heads a pioneering initiative established by the Kerala police called the Social Policing Division. It serves as a nodal office for all the social intervention campaigns of the force.

Over the course of my several interactions with IG Vijayan, I came across several other path-breaking social innovations he has designed. I would like to bring attention to these pioneering programmes that contributed to the institutionalisation of a changemaking culture across Kerala's schools.

Our Responsibility to Children (ORC): Most juvenile offenders are victims themselves—of broken families, economic deprivation, lack of education and much more. Thrusting them into the conventional police system has a greater chance of hardening them into career criminals than reforming them. The ORC project focuses on identifying children at risk and in need of care and attention, intervening with tailored support and integrating them into the mainstream by equipping and empowering them to become productive members of society. As part of this programme, more than 12,000 teachers were trained to follow a specially designed curriculum to enhance life skills, nurture strengths, address vulnerabilities and promote mentoring and good parenting.

Project Hope: This programme was initiated by the Kerala police and then made part of the activities of the Department of Women and Child Development. This project helps students who failed in Secondary School Leaving Certificate (SSLC) and Plus Two examinations to prepare better and qualify. A total of 2,426 students passed their exams in 2021-22 after being assisted under Project Hope.

Children and Police (CAP) House: This is a novel initiative based on the realisation that one of the fundamental duties of police is to create an invisible wall of protection around every child. CAP is a broad platform to strengthen the efficiency and reach of the initiatives mentioned above, so that abuse and violence against children are prevented and better protection and development are ensured to them. CAP facilitates constructive collaboration among police, various government departments, governmental and non-governmental agencies working for the welfare of the public and, most importantly, children. It recognises the fact that often problems faced by children go unacknowledged and unattended. Even if identified, they are rarely reported. In some cases, they are attended to very unscientifically, causing further damage. CAP House functions as a call centre, providing speedy information on various child-related matters, with the objective of providing support to various functionaries of the CAP initiatives as well as the public.

CHIRI: The pandemic-induced lockdown was a testing time for all, and its impact on children was severe. Depression and anxiety issues shot up before anyone could comprehend what was happening. Nearly sixty-six children killed themselves between the start of lockdown and its end in June 2020. It was in this context that the Chief Minister of Kerala launched the CHIRI Helpline under CAP House. The objectives of CHIRI, which in Malayalam means 'smile', are as follows:

- Develop a mental health support system for children in distress with the collective intervention of the relevant stakeholders responsible for the care and protection of children
- Identify and scientifically address the behavioural, emotional, interpersonal, learning and somatic challenges of children
- Promote general well-being of all children

Till October 2022, 34,588 calls were received through the dedicated CHIRI helpline number. Out of this 22,803 were enquiry calls and 11,785 were distress calls from the child or their parents. Mobile phone addiction (1,424), game addiction (1,355), mental stress (3,977), study problems (1,006), family problems (1,931) and lack of smartphones to attend the online classes (859) were the major issues reported by the children.

The CHIRI programme has helped more than 10,000 youngsters in distress in Kerala. As a result of the project, a network of psychosocial caregivers has been established across the state to provide services to children in distress. Specially trained female police officers respond to the calls, listening to the young callers and providing the necessary support and action. If the case is serious, the client's details are handed over to a mental health professional who adequately addresses the problem. The mental health professional is expected to reach the client over the phone within twenty-four hours. After twenty-four hours, an officer contacts the client to enquire if they received the service. If not, the professional is contacted again by the officer and they make sure the case is handled adequately. Later, the client is contacted by the officer to check with them on the status.

IG Vijayan has expanded the SPC motto 'We learn to serve' across multiple large-scale transformation projects for children. During the COVID-19 lockdown, SPC was one of the first responders that spread the light of positivity and explored possibilities of moving forward. It designed a bouquet of programmes to connect to children stranded during the pandemic and inspired them to stay positive.

The activities that the student cadets took up ranged from providing food to stranded people to creating a databank of more than three lakh blood donors through the Jeevadhara scheme to make up for shortage of blood in hospitals and blood banks. In another first, cadets organised Kutty Desk, a peer-to-peer telephonic platform to engage and support children cut out from social contact.

IG Vijayan is a visionary and a social impact guru who has shown us the pathway to convert the demographic advantage of India to a demographic dividend. He has championed youth empowerment by helping them to explore and expand their inherent potential. As a man who has touched millions of lives and transformed them through his various initiatives, he has become one of the extraordinary changemakers of our times—a changemaker who relies on the maxim #IAmTheSolution to collectively co-create with all a better tomorrow for everyone.

Acknowledgements

Our quest to chronicle the transformative impact of the remarkable social programme, the Student Police Cadet, begins by honouring the creator of this grand design. Our journey's genesis lies within the heart and mind of a visionary who not only conceptualised this unique program but also diligently materialized this concept into a palpable reality on the ground. To P. Vijayan IPS, we extend our deepest gratitude. His crucial support and commitment were integral in the realisation of this project and, therefore, the completion of our work.

We also extend our sincere appreciation to Loknath Behera IPS, the Kerala State Police Chief from 2016 to 2021, for his invaluable support. His approvals made it possible for our visits to SPC schools and interactions with the Kerala Police staff, enhancing our research for this book.

We are genuinely indebted to Saif Mohammed, a steadfast ally and guiding star during our explorations across Kerala. His untiring efforts to engage with cadets and collect their narratives, and his enduring commitment to the process have been fundamental in breathing life into this book. Saif, words cannot adequately express our thanks.

We had the privilege of Sreelatha Pillai's expert guidance, her advice on the book's framework proving invaluable. Ann Mary Chacko, through her scholarly pursuits on SPC, granted us a solid theoretical foundation for our narrative. Their contributions have been indispensable to our mission and we extend our heartfelt thanks to both.

Our publisher, Ajitha G.S., merits our deepest gratitude. Her ceaseless motivation, infinite patience, and grace enabled her to guide our project along its intended trajectory, despite our digressions and delays. Sanjana Tiwari meticulously polished our manuscript, spotting errors and bringing in her exceptional eye for detail, which greatly assisting in structuring the book. Jojy Philip has done an outstanding job with typesetting, working patiently with us on several changes. We are deeply thankful to them for their unwavering professional commitment.

Our thanks also go out to the dedicated officers of the Kerala Police Force involved with the SPC Programme, the committed teachers who poured their time and efforts into nurturing this initiative and, finally, to the inspiring students. These promising young individuals are carving out an exciting new landscape in youth empowerment. We dedicate this book to you—it is a testament to your endeavours as much as it is ours.

Our acknowledgements would be incomplete without expressing our gratitude to our families. Their unwavering and selfless support has been our safe harbour amidst a storm of uncertainties. To Sameera Rajan, Ameya Meera Anand, Amit Nandan, Akanksha Velath, Ganga Raj and Raj VK, your understanding and patience have been pivotal in helping us navigate the pressures and uncertainties encountered during the field research and writing of this book. Your roles, often unseen, were nonetheless essential. For that, we thank you sincerely, from the bottom of our hearts.

www.ingramcontent.com/pod-product-compliance
Lightning Source LLC
LaVergne TN
LVHW051221200726
843510LV00011B/1446